Praise for *Scary Close*

"The digital tools allowing us to act as our own publicity agent are making it harder, not easier, to connect. I'm thankful for Don who offers his journey out of 'public isolation' and into a life of intimacy. The work is hard but the reward is worth it. What a beautiful thing to be known."

Kirsten Powers, columnist, *USA Today*

"For those of us seeking a deeper happiness, *Scary Close* is a vulnerable, gripping, and impactful resource. Don provides a beautiful story and practical tools all in one transformational book. He stepped off the Grand Canyon of vulnerability in this one."

Miles Adcox, host, The Daily Helpline

"Since Donald Miller wrote this book, I expected it to be good. What I didn't expect was that *Scary Close* would completely transform my approach to my marriage, parenting, work, and faith. Everyone needs to read this book, but no one can have my copy. This is the one book I will be loaning to no one. I need *Scary Close* near me at all times reminding me that being a real, live, messy human being is miracle enough."

Glennon Melton, author, *Carry On, Warrior* and creator, Momastary

"Don invites us into his story of how he learned to impress people less and connect with them more. Finding connection is what everyone wants and yet we all struggle with it. Here's a friend who will walk alongside you as you fight for it, find it, and grow it. The journey is worth it all. Thanks, Don."

Henry Cloud, author, *Boundaries*

"Some authors I love because they're real, others because they're inspiring. Donald Miller is both. He has a way of drawing you into the narrative and then *bam!*, hits you with a truth you never saw coming. *Scary Close* will leave you feeling enlightened and refreshed and will change your relationships for the better."

Korie Robertson, *Duck Dynasty*

Scary Close

Also by Donald Miller

A Million Miles in a Thousand Years

Blue Like Jazz

Searching for God Knows What

Scary Close

Dropping the Act and Finding *True* Intimacy

Donald Miller

NELSON
BOOKS

An Imprint of Thomas Nelson

Published in Nashville, Tennessee, by Nelson Books, an imprint of Thomas Nelson. Nelson Books and Thomas Nelson are registered trademarks of HarperCollins Christian Publishing, Inc.

Thomas Nelson, Inc., titles may be purchased in bulk for educational, business, fund-raising, or sales promotional use. For information, e-mail SpecialMarkets@ThomasNelson.com.

Scripture quotations are taken from the Holy Bible, New International Version®, NIV®. Copyright © 1973, 1978, 1984, 2011 by Biblica, Inc.™ Used by permission of Zondervan. All rights reserved worldwide. www. zondervan.com.

In some instances, names, dates, location, and other details have been changed to protect the identity and privacy of those discussed in this book.

ISBN 978-0-7180-3567-9 IE

Library of Congress Control Number: 2014945329

ISBN 978-0-7852-1318-5

Printed in the United States of America

14 15 16 17 18 RRD 6 5 4 3 2 1

To Elizabeth Miller

Contents

Contents

Foreword

by Bob Goff

WE'RE ALL AMATEURS WHEN IT COMES TO LOVE and relationships. I've never seen anyone go professional, or wear a relationship jacket with stickers all over it from corporate sponsors like a NASCAR driver. They'll never make an Olympic event out of relationships either, although I can't lie, I'd like to see it in the winter games. We've let magazines on the end caps of our grocery stores, movies at our theaters, and old boyfriends and girlfriends who have failed us do most of the talking. Not surprisingly, we've ended up with a distorted idea not only of who we are, but also of what it means to love well.

Don Miller is one of my closest friends. I know that he loves me because he's told me. But even if he hadn't said a word, I'd know Don loved me because I have experienced how Don has treated me during times of tremendous joy, paralyzing sadness, and lingering uncertainty. In a word, He's been "with" me.

A number of years ago, Don and I went to Gulu, Uganda together. Uganda's civil war with the Lord's Resistance Army was still raging at the time and over a million people who had been displaced from their homes were living in displacement camps with no social services and very little security. When we arrived in Northern Uganda, we didn't stay in a hotel; we stayed in a camp with 38,000 displaced people. It was certainly more than a little unsettling. Abductions were still happening in the region by the LRA fighters. Most of these kidnappings were taking place in the displacement camps.

It was late in the evening before Don and I left the warm fire and conversation with leaders from the camp. In the dark, we made our way to the hut we were staying in. There wouldn't be any way to protect ourselves against any intruder who meant us harm. After ducking into a small opening in the hut, without saying a word, Don rolled out his mat in front of the door. They'd have to get by him to get to anyone else. Good friends do that; they guard each other when things get scary by putting themselves in between their friends and what could harm them. Don wrote this book with much the same in mind.

I GET A LOT OF MAIL. I BET YOU DO TOO. MOST OF mine is from people I know, but I get a fair amount of junk mail too. Before I open any of it, I check the return addresses to see if the mail is from someone I know and trust. Some of my junk mail is obvious and easy to pull from the pile and get rid of without reading it, but a lot of it pretends to look like it's not junk. Sometimes it's hard to tell the difference. The same is true in our relationships. This book will help you sort the junk mail you've been bringing to your relationships.

But if you're looking for a book with steps in it, this isn't the one for you. Don writes with intellectual honesty and sometimes-painful transparency about his own life. He's found honesty and transparency to be helpful guides. Don isn't asking us to agree with him about what he's experienced; however, he's challenged more than a few of my assumptions about what makes for good relationships and I'm better for it.

Don and I have spoken at quite a few events together over the years. The most difficult part for me is never who I'm talking to or what I'm talking about—it's introducing Don. If you can believe it, I've never made it a single time through introducing Don without getting choked up. I'm not really sure why. I think it's because I love Don and love makes us both strong and weak at the same time. I love who Don is, I love who he's becoming, and I am grateful for a guy who will put himself between me and what scares me the most, even if it costs him a lot.

Let me introduce you to my friend, Don Miller. And yes, I'm crying.

Author's Note

SOMEBODY ONCE TOLD ME WE WILL NEVER FEEL loved until we drop the act, until we're willing to show our true selves to the people around us.

When I heard that I knew it was true. I'd spent a good bit of my life as an actor, getting people to clap— but the applause only made me want more applause. I didn't act in a theater or anything. I'm talking about real life.

The thought of not acting pressed on me like a terror. Can we really trust people to love us just as we are?

Nobody steps onto a stage and gets a standing ovation for being human. You have to sing or dance or something.

I think that's the difference between being loved and making people clap, though. Love can't be earned, it can only be given. And it can only be exchanged by people who are completely true with each other.

I shouldn't pretend to be an expert, though. I didn't get married until I was forty-two, which is how long it took me to risk being myself with another human being.

Here are two things I found taking the long road, though:

Applause is a quick fix. And love is an acquired taste.

Sincerely,
Donald Miller

1

The Distracting
Noises of Insecurity

I DIDN'T START THINKING ABOUT MY HANG-UPS
regarding intimacy until my fiancée met me in Asheville
for a long weekend. I'd rented a cabin in the Blue Ridge
Mountains, where I was trying to finish a book before
we got married. I'd spent more than a year pursuing her,
even relocating to Washington, DC to date her, but once
the ring was on her finger I went back into the woods. I
wanted to finish the book so she wouldn't have to marry

a temperamental writer. No woman should spend her first year of marriage watching her new husband pace the floor in his boxers, mumbling to himself. The writing life is only romantic on paper. The reality is, what writers write and the way they live can be as different as a lump of coal and a diamond. The written life is shined to a deceptive gloss.

That's one of the problems with the way I'm wired. I don't trust people to accept who I am in process. I'm the kind of person who wants to present my most honest, authentic self to the world—so I hide backstage and rehearse honest and authentic lines until the curtain opens.

I only say this because the same personality trait that made me a good writer also made me terrible at relationships. You can only hide backstage for so long. To have an intimate relationship, you have to show people who you really are. I'd gotten good at reeling in a woman and then bowing to say, "Thanks, you've been a great audience," right about the time I had to let her know who I really was. I hardly knew who I really was myself, much less how to be fully known.

WHEN BETSY ARRIVED IN ASHEVILLE, I'D HARDLY talked to another human being in weeks. I felt like a scuba diver having to come to the surface when she asked a question.

We were sitting by the pond in front of the cabin when she asked how I could spend so much time alone. She said her friends admired my ability to isolate for a book's sake but wondered whether it was healthy. I don't think she was worried. She just found the ability foreign.

I thought about it and told her something I'd learned about myself in the year I spent pursuing her. I'd learned my default mode was to perform. Even in small groups I feel like I have to be "on." But when I'm alone my energy comes back. When I'm alone I don't have to perform for anybody.

She said I didn't have to perform for her. She didn't have to say that. I knew it was true. Who else do you marry but the person who pulls you off the stage?

BETSY'S EYES WERE AS GREEN AS THE REFLECTION of the trees on the pond. And as deep, I suppose. She was slow to trust, and even with a ring on her finger I knew part of her heart was being held back.

If I'm wired to impress people with an act, then Betsy is wired to withhold trust until it's been earned. She doesn't do it consciously. It's just that beneath her strong exterior there's fragility, so she doesn't offer her heart to just anybody.

Betsy told me when we met that in order to connect she needed quantity time. By that she meant we'd have to spend countless hours together doing nothing for her to feel safe. She believed anybody could come and go with a song and dance, but only the committed would last the seasons. And her community reflected this. While I'd spent my life getting people to clap for me, Betsy had laid a foundation with trusted friends, cousins, and siblings. And to those friends she was ferociously loyal.

In our year of dating, we'd only had one argument that was truly frightening. It happened after I insulted one of her friends. Actually, I rather objectively pointed out that one of her friends could be rude and might have a better chance with men if she'd stop emasculating them. I said I'd rather not spend any more time with that one, if she didn't mind. It turns out she did.

That single comment almost cost me our relationship. Betsy folded the napkin in her lap and set it on the table. She sat silently with murder in her eyes. When the waiter came to fill our glasses with water, I swear he backed away from the table without turning around.

And it wasn't even my comment that did it. It was the idea I could see a person as disposable. To Betsy, relationships were a life's work, the sum of countless conversations and shared experiences. She'd no sooner end a relationship than she'd cut down an old-growth tree. In the heat of that argument I realized I was only a sapling in the forest of this woman's life. I never spoke an ill word about one of her friends again. If I was going to win her heart, I'd have to plant myself in the forest and slowly grow the rings that earn loyalty, just as she and her friends had done with each other.

I knew then, this relationship would have to be different. I knew I'd have to know myself and be known. These weren't only terrifying prospects, they were foreign. I didn't know how to do either. And the stakes were high. I was going to have to either learn to be healthy or I'd spend the rest of my life pretending. It was either intimacy or public isolation.

ONE OF THE MANY GOOD THINGS GOD GAVE ME IN Betsy was the motivation to change. I'd spent years isolated and alone, working up words to tell people who I was—or more accurately, who I wanted to be. But in many ways that was a dark and lonely life. I'm not saying it didn't have its perks, because people clapping for you will always be a nice thing. But it's better when you have somebody to go home to and talk about it with, somebody who is more in love with you than impressed by you.

THAT'S THE GIST OF THIS STORY, I SUPPOSE. THESE are snapshots of the year I spent learning to perform less, be myself more, and overcome a complicated fear of being known. This book is about how I realized I could have a happy life without splitting an atom or making a splash. It's true our lives can pass small and unnoticed by the masses, and we are no less dignified for having lived quietly. In fact, I've come to believe there's something noble about doing little with your life save offering love to a person who is offering it back.

Here's a thought that haunts me: What if we are designed as sensitive antennas, receptors to receive love, a longing we often mistake as a need to be impressive? What if some of the most successful people in the world got that way because their success was fueled by a misappropriated need for love? What if the people we consider to be great are actually the most broken? And what if the whole time they're seeking applause they are missing out on true intimacy because they've never learned how to receive it?

Years ago, I remember seeing an interview with the son of a former president, who, after a sigh and a long silence admitted he'd spent countless hours with the most powerful man in the world but had no idea who he really was. "I never knew my father," the son said. "Nobody knew my father."

ONLY A FEW TIMES IN OUR LIVES DO WE GET TO know, in the moment, the impact of the moment itself. Robert Frost didn't tell us the fork in the road is easier seen in hindsight. But sitting there by the pond with Betsy I knew I could either let her really get to know me, or I could dance a jig and burn out like so much false love. And the decision would affect not only our relationship, but our future children's mental health, the lives of our friends, and perhaps, in some mysterious way, all of eternity.

I don't mean to overstate what is yet unknown, but part of me believes when the story of earth is told, all that will be remembered is the truth we exchanged. The vulnerable moments. The terrifying risk of love and the care we took to cultivate it. And all the rest, the distracting noises of insecurity and the flattery and the flashbulbs will flicker out like a turned-off television.

2

You Are Good at Relationships

THE FACT BETSY AND I WERE ENGAGED AT ALL WAS a miracle. Only a couple of years before we started dating I was convinced the only thing I had to offer in a relationship was pain. I'd broken off an engagement. I caused an enormous amount of damage, and the only positive was that the pain, both hers and mine, finally disrupted my pattern. I couldn't live this way anymore.

My pattern was this: I'd meet a girl who seemed

out of my league. I'd ask her out, spend time with her, start dating her, and then become obsessive. I needed her approval. It's not that I wanted it, I needed it. I'd wonder why she hadn't responded to my texts or my calls or why she didn't seem to like me the way I liked her. In my younger days, this killed any chance at a relationship, but as I got older I learned to hide it. I'd mark how many days on a calendar it had been since I made contact. I'd wait as many as ten before contacting her again so as not to look needy. I had a system and the system worked.

That's when phase two would kick in. Suddenly, after all that obsessing, I'd lose interest. I was drawn to girls who played the victim because girls who play the victim make you feel like a hero. Until you resent them. And after I couldn't stand them, I'd get mean. I'd say mean things. Then I'd feel bad and make up and then resent them again. My dating life was a death spiral of codependency and resentment.

And the last relationship was the most painful.

It was my friend Bob who finally convinced me to end it. Bob is a high-powered lawyer in San Diego, and he's skilled in mediating conflict. He sensed there was trouble from the beginning. He'd call every week or so to check in, to see how the engagement was going. And it was never going well. We'd be fighting again. Or I hadn't slept in days. She'd taken off the ring and stored it in a box. We'd canceled the wedding invitations.

"Don," Bob said, "I think this is over."

I had an office above a Thai restaurant on 23rd at the time. I leaned back in my chair with my feet on the windowsill. I thumbed through a pile of mail I hadn't looked at in weeks. He said it again. He said he thought the relationship was over and I needed to acknowledge the fact. I knew he was right. It had been over for months.

"Do you want me to get on a plane and help you tell her?" he asked sadly.

"No," I said. "I can do it."

So I did. It sounds trivial now. Millions of couples break off engagements and nearly all of them are better off because of it. But when you're in it, when you say all those words and don't mean them a couple months later, you feel like a fool. You wonder if your words have power anymore, and what is a man if his words are weakened?

Add to this the sadness, the confusing grief involved in hurting somebody and the forced realization there's something in you so unhealthy and careless it could level a heart.

My season of sadness lasted nearly a year. And once again, it was Bob who helped me through it. One afternoon when I was back in my office, trying to write, Bob called again. He asked how I was and I told him I would be fine. He asked how I was healing and I told him I was healing fine. Of course none of that was true. I wasn't fine at all. I was numb. I kept a bottle of whiskey behind a Bible on the bookshelf and when everybody went home I'd have three drinks and listen to music as a way of trying to feel something.

"You don't sound fine," Bob said.

I'd have argued with him, but I was afraid he'd notice I was slurring my words.

"You know what I've noticed about you, Don?" Bob said.

"What's that, Bob?"

"I've noticed you're good at relationships."

I said nothing. I wasn't sure I understood him correctly. Then he said it again, right into the silence of the phone.

"You're good at relationships, Don," he repeated.

The truth is I hadn't cried since I'd broken off the engagement. Like I said, I'd gone numb. But as he said those absurd words, something in me began to feel again and all the pain of the season swelled up. I pulled the phone from my ear, dropped my head on the desk, and wept. And as I cried, Bob kept repeating, "Don, you're good at relationships. You're still good at them. You've always been good at them."

For the next few months there was a yawning chasm between Bob's affirmation and the way I felt about myself. But he kept calling, and every time he'd call he'd say it again. "You know, Don, you're terrific at relationships. Remember that time you encouraged me? Remember that kid you and I met in Uganda and how much he loved you? Remember that girl you dated years ago who still thinks of you as a brother? We can't let our failures define us, Don. You're good at relationships, and you're only getting better." Like a trial lawyer he argued his case into my soul, week after week, until the chasm began to close and I started thinking about dating again.

When I say I started to think about dating again, I'm not saying I was ready for a serious relationship. Betsy didn't come around for another year, and God knows she'd have smelled my issues anyway. I only mean the pain subsided enough that I began to obsess again about girls. It was my same old pattern. But this time I recognized something was wrong. And I decided to get help.

3

Everybody's Got a Story and It's Not The One They're Telling

FOR YEARS I'D BEEN HEARING ABOUT THIS PLACE outside Nashville called Onsite. I'd heard it described as therapy camp for adults. I'd had several singer/songwriter friends who'd been stuck in their creative work and attended one of Onsite's programs and came back ready to write again. One friend, Jake, told me the program helped him figure out why he had so many screwed-up relationships. He said their workshops dealt a great deal with codependency and shame.

I signed up, but I really didn't want to go. I was mostly going because the breakup had been a bit public and I wanted people to know I was working on my issues. It's that old performer side of me, you know. Part of me believed that with time I could solve my own problems. I'd written best-selling books helping people resolve their issues, after all. Why couldn't I solve my own?

At the time, I was doing research on story structure, on the kinds of plots that make movies compelling. One day I realized something obvious: In all these movies, there was a similar plot. The hero is always weak at the beginning and strong at the end, or a jerk at the beginning and kind at the end, or cowardly at the beginning and brave at the end. In other words, heroes are almost always screwups. But it hardly mattered. All the hero has to do to make the story great is struggle with doubt, face their demons, and muster enough strength to destroy the Death Star.

That said, I noticed another thing. The strongest character in a story isn't the hero, it's the guide. Yoda. Haymitch. It's the guide who gets the hero back on track. The guide gives the hero a plan and enough confidence to enter the fight. The guide has walked the path of the hero and has the advice and wisdom to get the hero through their troubles so they can beat the resistance.

The more I studied story, the more I realized I needed a guide.

THE BUS RIDE FROM THE AIRPORT TO ONSITE WAS terrible. We'd flown in from all over, about forty of us, and we sat uncomfortably close to each other without talking. Even in my late thirties I felt like a teenager being sent to rehab. I looked around, wondering what the other inmates were in for. I tried to categorize them: pervs, cling-ons, pill poppers, conspiracy theorists. SkyMall must have made a fortune off these people during their flights.

When we arrived, I was surprised at the serenity of the place. Onsite is housed in an old mansion on a hill. Almost no other houses or farms are visible from the large front porch. Horses roam behind the mansion and a creek runs between the pasture and the neighboring hill. The staff is friendly, as though pretending they don't have a closet somewhere filled with tranquilizer guns.

Some of us had roommates at Onsite. When I asked the guy on the bed next to me what he was in for, he told me he came to Onsite because he'd destroyed his marriage and his company by telling lies. He said he didn't know why he lied, except he wanted to impress people. But he lied his way into bankruptcy and signed up for Onsite when his ex-wife told him about the place. Interestingly, I found the guy trustworthy after that. I felt like I could tell him anything. I didn't, but I felt like I could.

Our other roommate let us know, within two minutes of walking in the door, he was a master at Karate. He said he could get a guy on the floor in one move and snap his neck instantly. He made a swooshing sound as he described the move. Apparently when a neck breaks it makes a swooshing sound.

AT ORIENTATION THE ONSITE STAFF TOLD US WE had to turn in our cell phones. They said we could make a couple final calls if we needed to, but after that we wouldn't be communicating with the outside world for more than a week. Everybody scrambled to make their calls or check their stocks. I just put my phone in the basket. Who was I going to call? Bob? I could just hear him: "Don, you're great at rehab."

After we turned in our phones a guy named Bill Lokey came in and welcomed us. He had a slight Tennessee accent, wore a flannel shirt and jeans, and his thick, gray hair was parted and feathered back like a cleaned-up folk singer. He looked like a guy who'd stopped drinking decades ago and now read a lot of poetry.

We all sat down and Bill explained that years ago he'd ended his first marriage after having emotional affairs and living dishonestly. He said he'd come to Onsite, just like we had, where he learned about code-pendency and the unhealthy things people do to make themselves feel centered and whole. He said it had been a long journey but these days the temptations were gone. Years after leaving Onsite as a patient, Bill became a licensed therapist and came back to direct the programs.

MY FIRST BIG BREAKTHROUGH CAME WHEN BILL and I were having lunch in the mansion. I was making jokes and he asked if I knew where my entertainer gene came from. I couldn't believe he pegged me that quickly. I told him I didn't know, that I'd always felt a need to be smart or funny. He pulled a napkin from the table and drew a small circle on it. Inside the circle he wrote the word self and explained everybody is born a self. He said I was born this way and so was every-body else, a completely healthy and happy little self. And then, he said, something happened in my life that changed everything.

He drew a larger circle around the small circle, making something like a target. Inside the second circle he wrote the word shame. Bill said at some point I realized, whether true or not, there was something wrong with me. Either I didn't measure up to the standards of my parents, the kids at school made fun of me, or I came to believe I was inferior. Shame, he said, caused me to hide. "And that," he said, "is a problem. Because the more we hide, the harder it is to be known. And we have to be known to connect."

Then he drew another circle around the second one and said this outer circle was the false self we create to cover our shame. He said it was in this circle where we likely developed what we think of as our personality, or the "character" we learned to play in the theater of life. Bill said some of us learn we only matter if we are attractive or powerful or skilled in some way, but each of us likely has an ace card we believe will make us lovable.

Even before Bill asked me, I blurted out the word humor. So he looked at the napkin and wrote the word humor in the outer circle. He didn't look back up either. He just sat there with his pen hovering over a blank space in the outer ring. I said the word intelligence. And he wrote intelligence in the outer ring too.

I added a few more words and then we stopped. Bill turned the napkin toward me, and as I looked at it I felt as though I were looking at myself in a mirror. I was a self, covered in shame and hiding behind an act. Certainly it's not a black-and-white thing. I've no problem with a person being smart or funny, and I don't think it's wrong to receive validation in exchange for talent. But what Bill was getting at was deeper, a buried whisper within me that repeats a lie: I only matter if . . .

Bill pointed at the center circle, at the word *self*, and said, "This guy, your inner self, is the part of you that gives and receives love. The outer rings are just theater."

That night I went to bed wondering if my personality was largely a reactionary construct, a mechanism I used to gain respect from the world. In other words, what if my act wasn't who I was at all?

I had trouble sleeping that night. I wondered who the real me was, the me who was buried beneath those circles.

My roommates had trouble sleeping too. The guy who told the lies said he'd already broken down in one of the small groups. He said he missed his ex-wife and couldn't believe he'd thrown it all away.

I asked Karate if he'd learned anything that day and he was quiet for a while. He finally said he wasn't sure about all this sensitive stuff. He said his nature was to fight through everything. He got up to use the restroom, but when he did he didn't close the bathroom door all the way so some light slanted back toward his bed. My other roommate made a tapping sound to get my attention. I looked over and he pointed at Karate's bed. No kidding, right by his pillow was an old, worn-out teddy bear. Karate slept with a teddy bear. Unbelievable. I swear I loved the guy after that. Sometimes the story we're telling the world isn't half as endearing as the one that lives inside us.

4

Why Some Animals Make Themselves Look Bigger Than They Are

THE NEXT MORNING, BILL CHALLENGED US TO remember when shame had entered our lives. He said it wasn't likely we'd remember the exact moment, as shame had a way of forming even before we learned language.

But the further back we could remember, the more powerful the healing could be. He said acknowledging those early memories of shame and rewriting the story from a more gracious, adult perspective could help us heal.

We sat there in the big, open room on yoga mats with notebooks in our hands and thought. But I couldn't remember anything. I'd toughened over most of my youth. All my scars were now muscle, I supposed. For a while I considered the assignment a wash. Then, from the other side of the room, somebody started crying and writing in their journal. Then somebody else started crying and writing. You'd think peer pressure wouldn't affect you much after your school years but about the time Karate started sobbing I figured I better come up with something.

So I thought about my childhood. I suppose there had been a lot of reasons to feel shame. I'd been an overweight kid. I was terrible with girls. I couldn't dance. We were poor. My mother had sewn some of my shirts from leftover fabric my grandmother collected to make quilts. Still, all that stuff seemed comical. None of the awkwardness of growing up felt especially painful. But the more I listened to the other inmates sob, the more I considered there must be something more. And so I remembered something. The memory was preceded by a fear, as though my body were asking my mind to block it out.

It was a memory from elementary school. Sitting there on my yoga mat I remembered, for the first time in decades, I'd been a bed wetter most of my childhood. Seriously, none of the plumbing worked in my body until I was twelve. It felt like remembering another person. As though I'd lived multiple lives as multiple people and one of them had grown up with a small bladder and had spent his childhood wetting his pants at school. Could that really have been me?

But it was true. I'd spent the first five years of social interaction hiding from my peers. I navigated the halls of my elementary school holding my books in front of my crotch so people wouldn't see the pee ring. That was actually me. That was my story. It wasn't somebody else, it was me. I suddenly remembered spending the whole of one winter trying to pull my coat down over my crotch so nobody would know I'd wet my pants.

And then a specific memory came to mind. To this day, I think God invaded my thoughts right there at Onsite, in a safe place where I could receive the painful truth. I remembered a day when we had to walk to music class from our normal classroom. We lined up single file in the hallway and walked outside and across the playground to the separate classroom I normally loved, a classroom filled with instruments and choir risers and enormous posters with symphonies printed in music notes that looked as complicated as Morse code. But on that day I'd had an accident. I'd peed myself and was feeling anxious. In the normal classroom there were desks where I could hide my lap, but at music class we sat out in the open in a circle where all the other students could see.

As we lined up in the hallway my heart beat fast and hard as though pumping sludge. Even though it wasn't cold outside, I pulled my coat down over my crotch as we walked down the hall, into the outside courtyard and across the playground into the temporary buildings they'd turned into the music hall. When we walked in, the heat was turned up so high everybody took off their coats and piled them against the wall. I kept mine on. Our teacher instructed us to sit, but the chairs were uncomfortably close. She went to the piano and began teaching a song. I didn't sing. I was afraid that if I sang I'd blow my smell around the room. It wasn't long, though, before the kid next to me asked if he could move. He didn't say why. But soon enough there was an empty chair next to me and then, after another few minutes, the kid on the other side moved too. The room got quiet and a few children began to hold their noses. Some of the kids started to giggle and the other kids asked what they were giggling about. I said softly it was my coat. I said,

"A dog peed on my coat." Then another kid asked why I didn't just take off my coat. But I didn't want to take off my coat.

The teacher stood up and came around from behind the piano. I don't think she knew what to do. She said my name, softly. She asked if I wanted to step outside and talk about it. I said it was just my coat, that a dog had peed on my coat. She said my name again, very softly, and I stood up and said to the whole class that it was my coat, a dog had peed on my coat. I took off my coat and threw it in the pile with everybody else's coat but then realized the class could see my crotch. I ran out the door and across the playground and hid behind a tree. The teacher left the class and came and knelt and talked to me, but it was too late. My life was over and I was only seven.

That event happened decades ago. I know for some it's almost humorous. Perhaps it's because we were sitting on yoga mats or because everybody else was crying, but I swear I sat there and wept when I remembered it. I didn't care who saw or who heard, I just wept.

How a memory as startling as that had been lost for so long is a mystery. I knew in some ways I was still that kid. Like Bill said, I was a kid wearing a costume covering who I was, my flaws and my imperfections and my humanity.

I don't know why it felt so good to realize it, but it did. I was still that kid. And here's the other thing I suddenly realized: he was a good kid, a really good kid. I know he lied about the dog and I know he was awkward, but that was a good kid. Right there at Onsite I started crying, not because I'd peed my pants in school, but because I realized in running and hiding I'd sided with the other kids, I'd learned to believe there was something wrong with me. And it wasn't true. I might have been different, but there was nothing wrong with me. I was such a good little kid. I was annoying, I know, but I was basically a good little kid.

THAT STORY HELPED ME UNDERSTAND WHY I started developing an act in the first place. As soon as I found something I could use to cover my shame, I grabbed it and wore it around and in some ways felt like the real me was hidden behind a disguise.

It took years to develop the most recent act about being a writer, but I've had a few good ones along the way. I stayed invisible through elementary school and junior high, just trying to survive. Occasionally I encountered a bully, but mostly I avoided them. I'd say that was my first act, the invisible act. I didn't show my true self to anybody and I got terrific at not being noticed.

Some people manage to perfect the disappearing act well into adulthood. I went out with a girl once, years ago, who would disappear whenever there was conflict. Anytime there was tension she'd just go missing, and when I'd run into her again, or when I'd go over to her house to see what was going on, she'd be all chipper and act like everything was fine. Finally, one night when she was able to be vulnerable, she explained whenever she felt like she'd messed up she could close off that part of her mind and feel an inner peace that was completely disconnected from reality. She drove everybody else crazy because she couldn't resolve conflict, yet inside the false world of her mind everything was calm. And as crazy as it sounds, I understood her. I think she was doing the same thing I had done in junior high. She was climbing inside herself and going invisible.

My invisibility act worked great for years. But then I found something better.

WHEN I GOT TO HIGH SCHOOL, A MINISTER ASKED if I wanted to write an article for a church newsletter. When he asked, it felt like somebody had finally noticed me and wondered if there was something going on in my invisible world. I doubt that's exactly what he was doing, but that's the way it felt to me.

I spent a solid week on the article, all of four hundred words, no more than a few paragraphs. I gave it to the minister and he called and said it was good, that I was a good writer and smart. I still remember how I felt when he said the word smart. I felt a little drunk. Kind of disoriented. A pleasure chemical seeped into my brain and, without me knowing it, I'd become Pavlov's dog. If I was smart it meant I mattered. So I wanted to be smart.

When the article came out, people stopped me in the halls to say they enjoyed reading it. My mother told me she had friends calling to say they liked the article too. And that was all I needed. I had a costume and it felt great to wear it. I could be smart. I could write, and if I wrote I mattered. So for the first time I started reading books. And I kept writing. I heard a speaker quote a poem so I went home and started memorizing poems. I wrote more than a thousand poems over the next two years. And I started dreaming about writing a book.

Today, when people ask why I became a writer I try to answer honestly. I'm a writer because, at an early age, I became convinced it was the one thing I could do to earn people's respect. It's true in the process I learned to love words and ideas and these days I actually like to get lost in the writing process. But the early fuel, the early motivation, was all about becoming a person worth loving.

AT ONSITE WE BROKE INTO GROUPS TO WORK through some of our issues. We were talking about the false self when our therapist said something I found interesting. She said when some animals feel threatened they make themselves appear bigger. She said it's true with people too—they often make themselves appear better than they are in order to attract others and protect themselves from threats.

What she was saying was true, even for me while I was at Onsite.

The hardest rule for me to keep at Onsite wasn't about computers or cell phones. It was that we couldn't tell people what we did for a living. Bill asked us at orientation to keep our jobs a secret. He said if we had to talk about our work life, even during therapy, to just say we were plumbers or accountants.

It's a genius rule, if you think about it. Right from the start we weren't allowed to wear a costume. And let's face it, most of us wear our jobs like a costume. My entire identity—my distorted sense of value—came almost exclusively from the fact I wrote books.

It was torture to not tell people what I did. I never

realized how much I'd used my job as a social crutch until the crutch was taken away. I must have hinted that I thought my work was important a thousand different ways. I kept saying, "As a plumber, there's a lot of pressure on me to perform." I did everything but wink when I said it. I must have been nauseating to be around. But deep inside, I wanted so desperately to talk about what I did because I knew people would like me if they only knew. I knew people would think I was important. Slowly, over the week, I realized I was addicted to my outer shell, that without my costume I felt vulnerable.

I asked Bill if we would ever be able to share what we did for a living. He said we could, on the last day, right before everybody left. He said he learned people were going to share anyway, but they wanted to keep the group pure as long as possible. He also said when people finally revealed their jobs, it made him sad. He said friendships and relationships would develop over the intensity of the week, but when people learned some people made a lot of money and others didn't, or some people were slightly famous and others weren't, they divided into perceived categories. Interestingly, he said, it wasn't the rich who separated from the poor, but the opposite. He said people who didn't feel like they'd accomplished much felt insecure around those who had. Bill said he wished we lived in a world where people couldn't say what they did at all. He said the world would be a healthier place if nobody were allowed to wear a costume.

WHAT I FOUND CURIOUS, THOUGH, IS I BEGAN TO develop an entirely new personality during the week of therapy. My desire to be validated was that intense.

One night our small group got together just to relax. By then I'd come to really like this group and I wanted them to like me back. I was used to feeling special and set apart, but nobody in the group thought I was any better than anybody else—which was true, of course, but an attention addict is an attention addict. And then I caught my lucky break. One night when we were playing a board game in the parlor I happened to make a joke and everybody started laughing. They started laughing as though I were some kind of comedian. I felt that familiar high I get when I'm being validated. They approved of me. I stood out. I was special.

So I told another joke and then another and after that I got rolling. I was surprised at how sharp I could become when I had to, about how irreverent I could become if it got me the laugh. The entire group was in stitches. A few members of the group started demanding I tell them if I were a comedian in real life. And I started wondering if I'd missed my calling. I imagined leaving Onsite and working up a routine and maybe even leaving the writing life to become a stand-up comic. No kidding, the validation was that intoxicating.

WANT TO KNOW WHO DOESN'T THINK I'M FUNNY? Betsy. I can remember about five times when I've made her laugh, and God knows I've tried. The only way I can make Betsy laugh is if she's had a couple of drinks. I'm killer if she's tipsy. Mostly she sees my humor as a defense mechanism, though, a costume she has to put up with so she can have a relationship with the guy inside.

I heard once that Will Ferrell isn't funny to his wife and family. When I heard that I thought it was beautiful. It made me happy for him.

And yet this can be terrifying. I remember once when Betsy and I were hanging out with another guy she used to like and she kept laughing at his jokes. It was like he was throwing my ace cards around. Every time she laughed I felt like I was shrinking. And he was this dopey rock-climbing kid who wanted to be a fantasy football coach or something. He was ridiculous and I was way funnier, yet he made her laugh four times before we'd even ordered dinner. It was killing me.

But when we got back in the car at the end of the

night, she leaned into my shoulder and held my arm and I realized she'd liked the guy a lot—but she loved me. And as we drove home she held my hand and it was obvious she was having a bonding moment, as though all the pleasantness of the evening, even the other guy's humor, only meant something because she'd shared it with me. And for once I was glad I wasn't the guy doing the entertaining. Somebody else had to go back to the green room that night and obsess over his performance. I got to go home with the girl.

I began to wonder what life would be like if I dropped the act and began to trust that being myself would be enough to get the love I needed.

5

Three Things I Learned About Relationships From Swimming in a Pond

BACK IN ASHEVILLE BETSY AND I ENDED UP HAVING a great weekend. I rented a convertible in town and we visited the Biltmore Mansion and spent some time at Malaprop's Bookstore. We ate at Curate, a new restaurant where we taught the bartender to make a drink with whiskey, vermouth, and orange bitters. He liked it so much he said he might make it their fall cocktail. If you go to Curate, ask for the Don and Betsy.

The rest of the time we laid around by the pond and read our friend Shauna Niequist's book *Bread and Wine* and wondered what it would be like to someday own a bed-and-breakfast where we cooked all the recipes from Shauna's book. Shauna makes everything sound easy, including marriage, family, and pasta.

I'd be lying if I said our weekend in the mountains wasn't hard. I was used to being in DC, where I could go back to my apartment after our dates, sit around in my boxers, and watch television. In Asheville Betsy and I never left each other. What made me most uncomfortable were the awkward silences. Betsy says they're never awkward for her, but they are for me. When there's a silence in the conversation I feel like it's my responsibility to fill it. It's work, you know. I kept reminding myself the only way Betsy and I would make it is if I learned to trust her with those silences, if I learned to trust the reason she was marrying me wasn't to be entertained but to exchange love—that long, boring love that happens when a couple quietly eats cereal together while they read the paper.

After I dropped Betsy off at the airport I stopped at

Krispy Kreme for a doughnut. When I get nervous I eat sugar. I don't know what I was nervous about except the fear that I was about to commit to a lifetime of awkward silences.

The downside of being a writer is you get plenty of time to overthink your life. I like what Viktor Frankl wrote, about how we aren't designed to spend too much time thinking about ourselves, that we are healthier when we're distracted by a noble cause. But what do you do when the noble cause is a memoir? You sit around and think about yourself too much.

The only positive distraction I had in Asheville was the pond. Each day I'd go down and take a swim, letting the water distract me from my thoughts.

Thing One: To Be Intimate I'd Have to Jump

I WAS ON THE DOCK ONE AFTERNOON WHEN SOMEthing happened that helped me. From the dock you can look across the pond toward the mountains and it's beautiful. Water collects in a massive bowl of trees and rock that empties into the pond at the far end. There are no visible houses for miles and there's an echo about the place that confused my dog, Lucy, so badly she'd spend nearly every morning barking a conversation with herself. The pond is deep, about twenty-five feet in the middle, and the forest reflects on the surface so vividly it feels as though you could walk onto the water, as though it were the surface of a painting.

It was warm the evening Betsy left, and I wanted to take a swim. But as I walked to the end of the dock I felt a fear. I wanted to jump and didn't want to jump at the same time. I'd felt it before, back when Betsy and I swam the afternoon she'd arrived, but I didn't pay attention to it then. I just dove off the dock to impress her. But this time I studied the feeling. It reminded me of the fear I feel every year when I visit Bob's lodge. There's a cliff out in front of his house, about twenty-five feet or so, and every time I visit I make myself jump off, out past the rocks, into the water below. I never want to do it, but I feel like I have to. It's my yearly test.

Jumping off a cliff is one thing, but having the same kind of fear about jumping off the end of the dock had me confused. The dock was only a few feet off the surface of the pond. And it's not like the water was cold. I swam for an hour the day before. So why didn't I want to jump? Why was I having the same feelings I'd had at Bob's place, staring down from ten times the height?

Then it occurred to me what it was. I wasn't afraid to jump or to swim or to feel the sudden coolness of the water. I was afraid of change. On the dock I was warm and dry and in control. I knew once I jumped I'd be fine, I'd enjoy swimming around. But it was still a change. I thought about Betsy, likely about to land in DC. I knew in my heart I'd be happier with her. I knew she'd take me places that were healthier, more fun, more challenging than I'd ever been. I thought also about how content and comfortable I was being single, how much control I had in my life, how I could go out and get applause anytime I wanted and then retreat to the green room of my life, eating Oreos and waiting for my next performance.

I jumped off the dock. The water on the surface was cool and got colder as my body sank toward the bottom. I felt all the energy in the pond move into my muscles and when my head broke the surface it felt like a personal sunrise, as though the day were starting over. I breathed in the mountains and the trees and heard my splash come back at me from the hills. And the wind in the wooded bowl made the trees clap. I felt better in the water than I had on the dock. I thought about that, then, about how much I fear change, even change for the better. I thought about how there are so many lies in fear. So much deception. What else keeps us from living a better story than fear?

Later that week Bob asked me to Skype into his class

at Pepperdine Law School. The class was going through a life plan I'd created. I ended up Skyping in from the dock, the mountains and the cabin behind me in the video. I didn't tell them about the pond, though. For all they knew I was teaching from a lawn chair on the front lawn. I taught for a while and then told them the latest lesson I'd learned, that in order to experience a meaningful life, I'd have to face the fear of jumping in—not just in relationships, but in life, in our careers and our rest and our play. Then, fully dressed, I set my computer on the edge of the dock and did a cannonball into the pond. The class loved it. I'm not sure what any of it had to do with practicing law, but what good is practicing law if we don't love our lives?

Thing Two: Swimming a Little Is Swimming Enough

ONE OF THE REASONS I RENTED A CABIN WITH A pond is so I could get some exercise. I wanted to get into better shape before I got married. It's a big pond, large enough for an Olympian to work out if he or she were willing to swim in a circle. It's true that Betsy likes me how I am, but I do need to lose some weight and I figured swimming an hour or two a day would be enough to get started.

The first day I swam I was terribly out of shape. I could only swim hard for ten minutes or so and then had to get out for a break. After about three ten-minute swims I was done. Humbling, for sure. It wasn't long before I could swim a full workout, but I'd be lying if I said I enjoyed the routine. You'd think I'd be excited to get into shape, but I wasn't. I don't like to exercise, but not because it's painful or tiring. I've climbed mountains in Peru and ridden my bike across America. I'm willing. The reason I don't like exercise is because somewhere, in the deep recesses of my brain I've become convinced no amount of work is enough. I never leave a workout satisfied or proud of myself. And for that matter, I never quit a writing session thinking I've worked hard enough either. Or a teaching gig or a business meeting or anything else. I'm so bad about this I used to mow my lawn then crawl around on the grass with a pair of scissors, cutting uneven blades of grass. No kidding. I might have a problem.

There are really only two things a person can do when they're that much of a perfectionist. They can either live in the torture and push themselves to excel, or they can quit. I tend to go back and forth between the torture of working too hard and the sloth of quitting.

The reason I bring this up has nothing to do with exercise or writing. I bring it up because it's a symptom of a bigger problem, a problem that is going to affect mine and Betsy's relationship. The problem is this: those of us who are never satisfied with our accomplishments secretly believe nobody will love us unless we're perfect. In the outer ring Bill was talking about, the ring that covers shame, we write the word perfect and attempt to use perfection to cover our shame. I had a friend once who used to mumble curse words every time she drove by her high school algebra teacher's house because, years before, the teacher had given her a B-.

I think this all ties in with the entertainer gene. The root systems of these lies we tell ourselves tend to grow together. It's all connected with the belief human love is conditional. But human love isn't conditional. No love is conditional. If love is conditional, it's just some sort of manipulation masquerading as love.

Another argument Betsy and I got in was strange, for sure. She'd told me she loved me and rather than saying, "Thanks" or "I love you too," I made some kind of self-deprecating joke. She looked at me perturbed and ate another bite of her ice cream. I was offended that she didn't laugh, so I repeated the joke just to frustrate her.

"It's not funny," she said.

"It is funny," I said.

"No, Don," she said straightly. "When I say I love

you and you don't believe me, you're being a jerk. Basically what you're saying is I only love conditionally. You think you're being self-deprecating and funny, but you're really saying I'm not a good enough person to love you if you have a few flaws. It gets old."

I thought about her having said that when I was beating myself up for not swimming hard enough. If I was going to make Betsy happy, I'd have to trust that my flaws were the ways through which I would receive grace. We don't think of our flaws as the glue that binds us to the people we love, but they are. Grace only sticks to our imperfections. Those who can't accept their imperfections can't accept grace either.

I went back to the pond the next day. I jumped in and swam in a circle for twenty minutes or so, every muscle in my body burning. I stopped early and sat on the edge of the dock to catch my breath. I heard the voices, the deep feeling of dissatisfaction rising up. But this time I let it pass. Betsy needed me to be neither complacent nor perfectionistic. Those two poles were the death zones. So instead I congratulated myself on coming down to the dock to swim. I told myself the truth, that if I worked out a little every day for a year, I'd be in good shape. I asked myself if I wanted to keep working out. I didn't. Instead, I swam around the pond and threw a tennis ball for Lucy. I taught her to jump off the dock and even catch the ball in the air as she leaped into the water. And for the first time since I arrived at the cabin I felt relaxed. I wondered if Betsy wouldn't be more happy married to a man who was relaxed than a man constantly feeling like he wasn't working hard enough.

Thing Three: There Are More Lifeguards than Sharks

THE LAST THING I LEARNED ABOUT RELATIONSHIPS by swimming in the pond was there are more lifeguards than sharks. What I mean is, for the most part, other people aren't out to get us.

This fear of intimacy isn't something I was born with. When I was younger, even in high school, I could get quite close to people. In fact, some of the most intimate relationships I've enjoyed happened before I turned twenty-five. Since then it's been hit-or-miss. I'm not sure how it happened, exactly, but I think it's partly because I got mixed up with people who broke my trust. I've no awful stories to tell or anything, just a couple of bad business deals, a few scorekeeping relationships, and the occasional Twitter heckler. At some point, I just stopped trusting people. I began to believe everybody viewed life as a contest, a subtle version of Hunger Games. And to some degree I bought into the lie. If I needed somebody for something, I'd let myself get close but not too close, always keeping my parachute on.

I realized this was an issue I needed to work on just before I left DC. I was having lunch with my friend John Cotton Richmond. John is a human trafficking and civil rights prosecutor at the U.S. Department of Justice. He's the lead guy in the country taking down bad guys, those who enslave children and refugees and sell them in sex-trafficking operations. John is also one of the best husbands and fathers I know. He's like a real-life superhero, prosecuting the world's most evil criminals by day and kicking a soccer ball around with his kids the same night. And his wife adores him. He's one of the guys I'm hoping will guide me through the next season of life.

One afternoon while we were eating barbecue at Hill Country, just down from his office, I told him I'd had something of a breakthrough. I said I didn't think Betsy was out to get me. I said it seriously and with a straight face, but John started laughing. He nearly spit out his lemonade.

"Don, I would hope she's not out to get you. She's going to be your wife!"

I realized how absurd I sounded. I don't suppose I meant it to be accusatory. I only meant to say I was having a revelation that maybe people weren't as bad as I thought they were. And Betsy was likely the person who was convincing me this was true. I clarified to John that in the past I had assumed a woman would eventually try to control me, try to use me for something. But I wasn't sure people were really like that anymore. At least not all people. John laughed again. He looked down and shook his head, still smiling.

"I'm glad you had this revelation, Don," he said. "And I agree with you."

John paused in thought for a moment. "It's a tough question, you know. The heart of man. I've prosecuted some evil people." He looked at me sadly. "I'm talking about rapists and murderers. Leaders of child sex-trafficking rings. The works. And you want to know what they all have in common, Don?"

"What is it?" I asked.

"They all think people are out to get them. It's causing me to wonder if distrust doesn't bring out the worst in us. I know it's a complicated issue, because nearly everybody I put in prison has been tragically abused and so it's natural they don't trust others and they see life as a kill-or-be-killed drama. But it makes me wonder about those of us who deal with the same issue in lesser percentages. I wonder about my own heart. Am I willing to be hurt occasionally and turn the other cheek in order to have a long-term, healthy relationship?"

John looked me in the eye and said, "I think you're on to something here, and it's good. I think the risk of trusting Betsy is worth the reward of intimacy."

Since talking to John that afternoon I've noticed something interesting. The harshest people I've met over the years have had two things in common: they don't fully trust anybody, and they view relationships as a means to an end.

I read an article a few years ago about Apple Computers' retail division and the way they do customer service. They want their team members to trust the "positive intent" of their customers. So when a customer comes in with a complaint, they don't want their team members to assume they are trying to rip off the company or get something for free. They know the occasional loss will be offset by the connection they create with their customers by trusting them.

Trusting people is a slow and natural process, I know. But it's already paying off. I've noticed the more I trust Betsy the gentler my own spirit becomes. My trust for her is changing me.

BEFORE BETSY LEFT THE CABIN WE WERE LYING ON the dock, looking at the clouds and having one of those awkward silences that are still difficult for me.

Thinking we had to talk to connect, I asked her if she'd rather swim in a pool, a lake, or the ocean. Betsy sat up, dangled her feet off the dock, and said she'd rather swim in the ocean. She grew up going to Florida with her cousins and they'd spend the entire day playing in the waves, poking jellyfish with sticks and eating peanut-butter-and-jelly sandwiches with sand in them. She and her cousins would lie in bed at night and giggle because they could feel their bodies lifting and falling as though they were still in the waves. Those were some of the greatest days of her life.

She asked whether I would rather swim in a pool, a lake, or the ocean. I said I'd rather swim in a lake. "Why?" she asked. I said in a lake you didn't have to deal with the jellyfish and the seaweed and the sharks and whatever else. Betsy thought about that for a moment then reminded me that trying not to get stung by a jellyfish was part of the adventure.

Betsy ran her fingers through my hair and kissed me on the forehead. I told her I'd put some jellyfish in the pond if she wanted me to.

"It's worth it to get stung by a jellyfish every once in a while," Betsy said. "For the occasional sting, you get to go to sleep feeling the waves and you get to giggle with your cousins."

I doubt she realized it, but she was talking about

much more than the ocean. She was talking about what it meant to risk yourself on love. It meant diving into the unknown, where there were very real dangers, but mostly rewards.

6

Performance Anxiety
in Real Life

LIKE I SAID, THE REASON I RENTED THE CABIN WAS so I could finish a book. I might have been able to finish it back in DC, but I wasn't sure. And I knew I had to finish the book. Or, more honestly, the broken wound inside me knew I had to finish the book. I'll explain.

After Betsy left Asheville I was feeling lonely but also a little stressed. The book wasn't coming along like I wanted. And I was staring at a calendar, knowing my days were numbered. If I couldn't wrap up the book within the next four weeks, I'd almost certainly lose traction on it because I was going into a season of speaking. I'd accepted a bunch of teaching gigs to pay for the rehearsal dinner and honeymoon.

That kind of pressure is no good for me. I write best when I'm relaxed, when I'm sitting across from the reader and having a casual conversation. Forcing the words doesn't work. At least not for me.

It so happened the afternoon I was feeling the pressure Ben Rector put out a new album. Ben's a favorite of mine and Betsy's. We're crazy fans.

Anyway, I downloaded Ben's album and was listening to it on the porch, when a song came on I'd never heard before. The song was called "Making Money." It sounded like an old Billy Joel song, as though he'd sat down at the piano and wrote a late-night journal entry. He'd recently encountered success and life was changing. He wondered whether some aspects of the new life were worth it.

> *Making money isn't easy*
> *And it sure won't make you happy*
> *So I think it's funny*
> *We're so concerned with making money.*
> *And money won't keep folks from grieving*
> *And it won't stop love from leaving*

So here's my two cents
What's the use in making money?[*]

Maybe it's because I'd had a whiskey, or because the rain was exceptional coming in off the mountains, or because I was missing Betsy so terribly, but that song leveled me. I just sat there, fully realizing why I was so far away from the woman I loved. I was far away from Betsy because I secretly believed if I didn't finish the book and stay slightly famous, or if I didn't make money, or if other people didn't think I was a success, then she'd have no reason to love me.

I knew it wasn't true, but what our head knows our body often defies. My stress, my sense of urgency, my worry at night about whether the book was coming along had to have been coming from somewhere, and the place it was coming from was this place of severe worry that if I'm not impressive I won't be loved.

But the truth is, Betsy doesn't care about money, and the fact I'm a known author was a massive hurdle I had to overcome to date her. She assumed I was full of myself, which I guess was partly true.

Regardless, if I spend the rest of our marriage

---

* Download Ben Rector's "Making Money" on the free Scary Close Soundtrack at www.scaryclose.com

believing she won't love me unless I succeed, our marriage will be a disaster. God is going to reveal me as a flawed human being as fast as he can and he's going to enjoy it because it will force me to grapple with real intimacy.

Somewhere along the line I think many of us buy into a lie that we only matter if . . . We only matter if we are strong or smart or attractive or whatever.

It makes me wonder if this isn't the reason I've struggled with a kind of performance anxiety. I'm not talking about the kind of anxiety you get before you have to give a speech or something. I'm talking about the fact I'd rather be alone or with a close friend than have to make small talk at a party. It's exhausting to me and I feel like I'm acting in a play about life every time I have to do it.

I can trace my need to perform and impress people back to some of my earliest memories. Dad left just as I was coming into my own, I suppose—and my mother, sister, and I were feeling abandoned and neglected. In a way, being the only male, I felt like I had to be a bit bigger and better of a person than I was. This was foolish, of course, but kids don't process reality objectively.

So it was during this season I developed a strange desire to convince people I was intelligent. For whatever reason, it became important to prove to my mother and sister, not to mention friends of the family, that I was smart and could handle things.

The problem is, I wasn't exceptionally smart. I hated school, had no interest in books, and never did my homework.

I remember seeing a kid profiled on *60 Minutes*, a kid who had autism and could play any symphony on the piano after hearing it once. I was insanely jealous. After several loud and failed attempts on the piano at church, I realized I'd have to find another path.

Occasionally I'd be asked a question and rather than answering immediately I'd roll my eyes back in my head as though trying to read some bit of information I'd stored in photographic memory.

"What kind of sandwich do you want?" I'd be asked.

I'd widen my eyes trying to convince the babysitter I had the mind of a savant. "Peanut butter and jelly," I'd say after rolling my eyes back to normal. She would stand there looking at me as though we were having a powerful moment, a moment I misinterpreted. More than one babysitter thought I'd been possessed by a demon.

Once, on the morning of my sister's birthday party, I cleaned my room and found an old tape recorder buried in the closet. Before anybody showed up for the party I got a screwdriver from the junk drawer and took the tape recorder apart, spreading the pieces across my bed. I had no idea what any of the parts were called or how they created a tape recorder, but I laid them out as though I understood, and when my sister's very cute friends finally showed I pretended to be putting it back together. I'd pick up a part and they'd ask what it was and I'd work the screwdriver pretending they were bothering me and tell them they wouldn't understand, that it had to do with electronics. They'd shrug their shoulders and prance off, their bouncy hair looking shiny in the corner of my eye.

This is another early memory of projecting an identity that wasn't true. I suppose I've been doing it ever since, only I've gotten more sophisticated in my attempts. These days, I'll spend weeks in a cabin, writing and rewriting chapters so they seem effortless.

Partly, that's the job of a writer, but the reality is all writing is a subtle form of manipulation, not always malicious, but usually designed to do two things: (1) communicate an idea and (2) make the writer sound intelligent.

I LEARNED A LOT ABOUT WHERE MY PERFORMANCE anxiety comes from when I continued to meet with the therapist after OnSite. Bill said it would be important to keep working on the ideas we uncovered, so I did.

She was a delightful woman, recommended by a

friend. She was old enough to have retired years before but loved people and loved counseling and only took on enough clients so she and her husband could go on cruises together several times each year. Whenever we'd meet, she'd have to force herself to stop talking about whatever cruise they were planning next. They'd been to Turks and Caicos, Alaska, Bermuda—and they'd been to Hawaii four times. The second time we met she even brought me a brochure. She said I'd be the youngest person on the boat by about thirty years but I really ought to look into it. And honestly it sounded great. A week at sea eating anything I wanted, betting a quarter at a time at the blackjack table, and being in bed by nine thirty sounded like a lovely life. Especially the way she described it. She and her husband had done their work, both physically and emotionally, and it was as though they'd finally woken up to the fact we were meant to enjoy life, not be drowned by it.

ANYWAY, WHEN WE ACTUALLY STARTED THE COUN-seling part, she helped me have a breakthrough. She put a giant piece of butcher paper on the wall and drew the shape of a person with a large head and large body. Then she drew the shape of an even larger person around the outside of the first person. She said these two shapes represented my internal and external self. She then asked me to write some adjectives inside each shape. Inside the smaller me I wrote gentle, calm, knowing, responsible, wise, and so on, all words that kind of surprised me because they were so positive. It turns out my internal self was doing pretty well. And then in the outside person I wrote show-off, desperate, anxious, funny, charming, tired, words that also surprised me. Turns out my outer self was feeling pretty stressed. No wonder I was more comfortable alone than I was with people.

I sat down and we looked at the drawing together. She seemed to realize exactly what we were looking at. She said, "Don't you see how interesting this is?" I told her I had no idea what it meant.

So she stood up and took two chairs and faced them toward each other. She said one chair represented who I was internally and the other chair represented who I was externally. She asked me to sit in the chair that represented the inner me and then she asked me how it felt. I said I felt great, that I was calm and at peace. She asked me how old I was, not my real age, but the age I felt while sitting in the chair that symbolized my inner life. I thought about it for a second and told her I felt like I was about thirty-five, old enough to have figured life out and yet young enough to still build something I could work on for decades. "Great," she said. "Fascinating."

She then asked me to sit in the chair that represented the external me. I stood up and walked over to the other chair. I noticed immediately I felt a little anxious, confused, and pressured and I told her so. She said, "Don, how old are you in this chair?"

"I'm nine." I said. "I'm nine years old." She just sat there and let me think about it for a moment. I know this sounds odd and goofy, but in one chair I really felt like a capable adult and in the other I felt like a scared kid.

"Don," she said, "do you realize you're sending a nine-year-old out to do all your performing?"

What my counselor said made complete sense. Ever since I was a child, ever since I became wrongly convinced I had to be bigger and smarter than I really was, I've been trying to perform, trying to convince people I was more capable than I really was. I'd been sending that same nine-year-old kid who took the tape recorder apart out into the world to speak and perform and interact with people.

She asked me to come back and sit in the adult chair and tell the nine-year-old what I thought about him. I didn't know what to say. She asked me to imagine what he looked like, and I immediately pictured the chubby kid from the movie *The Goonies*. I smiled. I liked the kid. He was funny and disarming and yet still only nine years old. He seemed alone and afraid, and the only way he could get attention was to convince everybody around him he was smarter and stronger than he actually was.

My therapist asked me, again, to say something to him. I looked at him for a while and he looked back, wide eyed and curious. I finally spoke up and said I liked him. I told him I thought he was funny and charming and smart.

"Anything else?" my therapist said.

"Yeah," I said. "I also want to say I'm sorry. I'm sorry for pushing you out there in the world so you could impress people for us and fight for us and make money for us while I sat in here and read books."

The moment was powerful for me. I'd completely disassociated from the kid who had taken apart his tape recorder. I hardly knew him. I'd not raised him to maturity and he'd spent the last thirty years lonely and desperate for attention. It's no wonder I hid from the world. It's no wonder parties made me tired or I got exhausted after I spoke. It's no wonder criticism made me angry or I overreacted to failure. I think the part of me I sent out to interact with the world was, in some ways, underdeveloped, still trying to be bigger and smarter as a measure of survival.

I LOVE THE ITALIAN MOVIE *WE HAVE A POPE* BY Nanni Moretti. It's a beautiful, slow-moving film that takes place inside the Vatican. At the beginning of the story, the College of Cardinals comes together to choose a new pope, as their current leader has passed away. Ballot after ballot is cast, but the cardinals can't come to an agreement. Finally a cardinal named Melville is chosen and in a rather moving scene, he timidly, almost reluctantly, accepts the responsibility.

Burdened with feelings of inadequacy, he declines to stand on the balcony and be formally announced as the new pope. Instead, he retires to his apartment to pray. The crowd of one-hundred-thousand-plus people in St. Peter's Square is told the announcement will be made the following day. But the new pope refuses to leave his apartment. He's paralyzed by fear.

As the story progresses, the cardinals dress the new pope in street clothes and smuggle him from the Vatican to see a psychoanalyst, a woman who has no idea who he is or what responsibility has been cast upon him.

The scene is subtle but terrific. The counselor is asked to help the man, but Pope Melville is told he can't reveal his true identity or the reality of his circumstance. She asks what the man does for a living. Melville sits in silence until he realizes a way to explain what he does without revealing who he is. He says to the counselor: "I am an actor." His answer reveals it all, that his job is to confidently play a part that may or may not be related to who he actually is as a person.

I can't tell you how much I identify with that answer. I am an actor. I play a role.

From the counselor's office, Melville escapes from the Vatican officials and walks the streets of Rome. Perplexed, he enters an outdoor market and wonders at the complexity of the world that would soon be his charge to serve. He attempts to escape the frightening reality by attending a play, but he is found. Vatican officials march into the theater where he is hiding, shut down the play, and pull the cardinal from the crowd to return him to the Vatican.

Under much pressure, the cardinals prepare the new pope for his announcement. They dress him and review the lines he will read on the balcony. His hand is shaking. The other cardinals are praying. He does not want to go.

Then suddenly we see peace come over him. He has had a revelation.

The crowd in St. Peter's Square is an ocean of hopeful parishioners. The new pope walks onto the balcony and the crowd erupts. It is Melville. He stands silently for a short time, taking in the scene, then finally folds his notes, leans to the microphone, and declines the assignment to become pope. He says the cardinals have chosen the wrong leader.

The other cardinals gasp in embarrassment at the

announcement, but Cardinal Melville breathes easy. His personal conclusion is implied: He doesn't want to be an actor, nor does he feel it necessary to act in order to serve God.

Nanni Moretti took heat in Italy for making the film. Some considered it a criticism of the papacy. But I didn't take it that way. To me, it was a human story about what it costs to be yourself, and the reward too. It costs personal fear to be authentic but the reward is integrity, and by that I mean a soul fully integrated, no difference between his act and his actual person. Having integrity is about being the same person on the inside that we are on the outside, and if we don't have integrity, life becomes exhausting.

I wonder how many people get tempted by the gains they can make by playing a role, only to pay for those temptations in public isolation.

THE REALITY OF TRYING TO BE BIGGER AND smarter than we are is that it sort of works, and then falls apart. It's true people are attracted to intelligence and strength and even money, but attraction isn't intimacy. What attracts us doesn't always connect us. I can't tell you how many friends I have who have been taken in by somebody sexy or powerful or charming but soon after find themselves feeling alone in the relationship. It's one thing to impress people, but it's another to love them.

BACK IN ASHEVILLE, SITTING ON THE DECK WATCH-ing the rain and listening to Ben Rector, I realized what Betsy needed was me. And I had to trust I was enough. She didn't need my money or my power or anything else. Some of that might be temporarily attractive, but none of it would create intimacy. She needed me.

I remember when Betsy and I first spoke about getting engaged, back when we realized we had to make plans and put things on calendars and figure out what the next year looked like. In a somewhat serious moment, Betsy said she didn't care what kind of ring I bought, and she really didn't care how I proposed. "But," she said, "please don't involve a Jumbotron at a ballpark." I laughed. "I'd never," I said. She smiled and wiped her brow.

There were plenty of times after that we ended up at the ballpark watching the Nationals, and we even made it to the Seahawks game when they came to play the Redskins. I always joked that any moment I was going to take a knee. She rolled her eyes and said I'd better be tying my shoes.

It's funny, looking back, but those ballpark jokes told me a lot about the woman I was about to marry.

She didn't want to be in a running show about romance. She's not a performer. Betsy wants to connect. What speaks love to her isn't money, power, or fame. It's a phone call in the morning to pray about our day, a text-message to say I'm thinking of her, a handwritten note, a postcard when I'm out of town on business, remembering what drink she likes when we're at a bar, asking follow-up questions about her friends, and not hiding behind humor when it's time for a serious conversation. And the reality is, none of that is difficult. It just requires being thoughtful and seeing the world, at least in part, from her perspective. It doesn't require acting. It just requires being myself and showing up.

Much of the time I've spent trying to impress people has been a waste. I'm grateful, in some ways, because my insecurities fueled my career, but I'm beginning to realize the adult part of me and the child part of me need to come together and create a whole human being capable of intimacy. And all this makes me wonder if the worry and doubt I've experienced about being lovable wasn't unfounded.

The reality is people are impressed with all kinds of things: intelligence, power, money, charm, talent, and so on. But the ones we tend to stay in love with are, in the long run, the ones who do a decent job loving us back.

7

The People We Choose to Love

ONE OF THE TRUTHS I PICKED UP FROM JOHN
Cotton Richmond, my friend at the Department of
Justice, is that some people are not safe. John has the
emotionally difficult job of putting serious criminals
in jail, but criminals who also have been victims themselves earlier in their lives. And while he has compassion
for their stories, he also realizes the community needs
to be protected from them.

I have no idea why one person can be handed a tragic past and become healthy and selfless while another amplifies their pain into the lives of others. Almost without exception the most beautiful, selfless people I've met are ones who've experienced personal tragedy. They remind me of the trees I occasionally stumble across in the Columbia River Gorge, the ones that got started under boulders and wound slowly around the rock face to find an alternative route to the sun.

What's harder for me to admit, though, is there are also people who've become the very rocks that hindered them. And perhaps there is redemption for these people and perhaps there is hope, but this doesn't change the fact they are not safe. I only say this because a positive evolution happened in my life when I realized healthy relationships happen best between healthy people. I'm not just talking about romance either. I'm talking about friendships, neighbors, and people we agree to do business with.

One of the things I admire most about John is his ability to hold compassion in one hand and justice in the other. He offers both liberally and yet they don't cancel each other out.

I remember talking to my friend Ben once about a person who had once lied to me. We'd been working on a project together, and this person lied about some of the finances. Ben is a decade older than me, a cinematographer with a gentle heart, a guy you'd think could easily be taken advantage of. But when I told him about my friend, Ben said, "Don, I've learned there are givers and takers in this life. I've slowly let the takers go and I've had it for the better." He continued, "God bless them, when they learn to play by the rules they are welcomed back, but my heart is worth protecting."

At first, it was hard to act on what Ben was talking about, about the givers and the takers. I felt like a jerk for letting my friend go. But then I realized I didn't have a healthy relationship with him in the first place. When there are lies in a relationship, it's not like you're actually connecting. And I realized another thing too: it wasn't me who was walking away from my friend. It was my friend who hadn't played by the rules and was incompatible in a healthy relationship. And here's another thing that's strange. After distancing myself from my friend I loved him more, not less. I protected myself for sure, but my anger went away. Once he wasn't hurting me anymore, I could finally have compassion and grace.

It makes me wonder how many people have damaged their own lives by mistaking enablement for grace?

I REMEMBER YEARS AGO, HEARING A BIBLE STORY in church about a married couple who tried to run a con on their community. A man named Ananias sold some land and donated some of the profits to the church, but he lied and said he'd given them all the money. God killed him on the spot. Seriously, he dropped dead right after he lied to the community. Later, not knowing about her husband's death, his wife came in and ran the same con, only to drop dead too. The issue wasn't whether or not they gave all their profits—plenty of people likely didn't. The issue was they'd lied to their community.

I remember another story from church. I remember a story about Jesus meeting a rich man and really liking him. Jesus invited the man to go with him, to sell all his stuff and follow him. The rich man really wanted to go but didn't want to sell his stuff. Jesus looked at the man and loved him. Jesus didn't berate the man or chastise him but actually stood there and felt love for him. But in the end they went their separate ways.

I used to think that story was about the dangers of wealth, and to some degree I suppose it is. But I also think it's a story about boundaries. Jesus didn't give up his purpose and community and calling to swim in the rich man's pool or vacation with him in Spain.

I think that story about Jesus and the rich man also

means that while everybody is invited, not everybody is willing.

I SAW A *60 MINUTES* EPISODE RECENTLY WHERE Morley Safer interviewed the actor and illusionist Ricky Jay. He's a sleight-of-hand guy. You'd recognize him if you saw him. He's been in dozens of movies, mostly playing character bits. But what he's best at is misdirection. He can blow your mind with a deck of cards. He sells out packed houses, doing trick after trick with his fifty-two assistants. In the interview with Morley Safer, he talked about having predicted the Bernie Madoff scandal. He pulled a piece of paper from a file and explained he'd delivered it to the authorities months before Madoff was caught. He said he told the authorities to look out for three things: for returns on investments far above average and with such frequency that investors will hesitate asking for a return of their principal; for somebody who will rely heavily on an affiliation with an investor group be it religious, ethnic, or geographic; and finally, somebody who makes it difficult to invest with them, who appears to be disinterested in money and makes people seek them out rather than vice versa.

Long before the Madoff scandal was exposed, a

sleight-of-hand guy predicted the whole thing. Why? Because he was a master manipulator. He knew the tricks. Remarkably, though, Morley Safer fell for it. He thought Ricky Jay was a genius. Then Ricky Jay revealed he had conned Morley Safer, too, because he'd written the whole thing the night before the interview, printed it on a piece of paper, and put it in a file so he could bring it to the interview. Ricky Jay hadn't predicted Bernie Madoff's crimes at all. A con man is a con man is a con man. At least Ricky Jay was honest in the end.

I respect Ricky Jay, but I don't respect him because he can run a good con. I respect him because there's something in him that wants to confess, wants to reveal his tricks, wants to connect with people. It's true the manipulator is the loneliest person in the world. And the second loneliest is the person being manipulated. Unless we're honest with each other, we can't connect. We can't be intimate. Only God can penetrate a manipulative person's heart, and even then, he sits quietly, waiting for them to stop running their con.

A YEAR OR SO AGO I READ AN ARTICLE THAT SAID in the next five years we will become a conglomerate of the people we hang out with. The article went so far as to say relationships were a greater predictor of who we will become than exercise, diet, or media consumption. And if you think about it, the idea makes sense. As much as we are independent beings, contained in our own skin, the ideas and experiences we exchange with others grow into us like vines and reveal themselves in our mannerisms and language and outlook on life. If you want to make a sad person happy, start by planting them in a community of optimists.

After I read that article I got pickier about who I spent time with. I wanted to be with people who were humble and hungry, had healthy relationships, and were working to create new and better realities in the world.

THE OTHER DAY I WALKED INTO A RESTAURANT TO get some work done and ran into my old friend Thad Cockrell. He's a rock star, sort of. He's the lead singer of a band called leagues, and Betsy and I love their music. I went over and said hello and asked how he was doing. He was honest. He said he wasn't doing too well. "Why?" I asked. He motioned for me to sit down.

Thad sighed and kind of laughed and said, "Don, I'm lonely."

"Lonely?" I said.

"Yeah, lonely," he repeated.

It was a little odd. The guy has had more than a few girlfriends and could likely walk away with any girl in the restaurant. But he said he wanted more, he wanted to settle down and have somebody to take care of. He said it had been tough, though. Most of his relationships had crashed and burned and left him with a broken heart. "It's great for the music but terrible for my soul," he said.

I recognized his predicament. He was me, only a couple of years before. "Thad," I said, "can I ask you something?"

"Sure," he said. "As long as you don't put it in a book."

"I'll change your name to Ralph," I promised.

"Ask away," he said.

"Ralph, I said, are you drawn to drama?"

He started laughing as soon as I asked. "Is it that obvious?" he said. I told him it wasn't obvious but sometimes when a person gets into a bunch of relationships that crash and burn, they're drawn to drama.

Then I told him something my friend John Cotton Richmond once said to me, that 90 percent of people's problems could be prevented if they'd choose healthier people to give their hearts to.

Ralph looked at me, curious. "What's a healthy

person?" he asked. I told him I was still figuring that out myself, but I'd not met a lot of healthy people who were dramatic.

The reality is this, though: a healthy person coupled with an unhealthy person will still result in an unhealthy relationship.

HERE'S A TRUE STORY I HAVEN'T TOLD YOU. WHEN Betsy and I first met she wasn't interested in me, because she sensed I wasn't healthy. No kidding. We knew each other nearly five years before we started dating. I liked her immediately. I'd send her an occasional e-mail and when I was in DC we'd get together for coffee. While she was polite, she never led me to believe she was interested. And she wasn't.

It wasn't until I began to change that Betsy started thinking of me as more than a friend. We got together for dinner one night and caught up and I told her about Onsite, about the work I'd been doing and about how I was taking a break from dating. I told her I was trying to figure out what it means to be in a healthy relationship. It wasn't the kind of speech most women would be drawn to, but Betsy was intrigued. I think she'd been around so many guys trying to impress her that the truth piqued her interest.

When I was done taking my break from dating I called and asked her out. She agreed. We dated long-distance for a season. I'd fly out to DC for a weekend, and the next month she'd come visit me in Portland. After a while, though, I began to repeat old habits.

Back in those days, I'd manipulate women by talking about marriage well before the relationship had been tested. I did this to reel the girl in and get a sense of security, at which time I'd lose interest.

But Betsy didn't fall for it, nor did she let it scare her. She just explained it didn't seem healthy for us to talk about marriage yet. While I was tempted to get defensive and dramatic, I realized she was right. Sooner or later the stuff I'd learned about healthy relationships kicked in and I began to trust the slow and natural process of learning to love and be loved by another person.

I'd be lying if I said our relationship was as exciting as the unhealthy relationships I'd been in in the past. It wasn't. But I'd lost the taste for drama. The backside of Hollywood passion is disappointment and loneliness—and more often than not, resentment and cynicism about the nature of love itself.

Betsy and I were building more of a symphony than a pop song.

Don't get me wrong. Love is wonderful and our getting to know each other was the harvest of a long season of farming. But true intimacy is just like that: it's the food you grow from well-tilled ground. And like most things good for us, it's an acquired taste.

8

Control Freak

AFTER REALIZING WE BECOME LIKE THE PEOPLE WE spend time with, I decided to hang out with better people. I had a friend across town named David Price who was married to a great woman and ran his own business analyzing data for large companies. Before he analyzed data, though, he worked for an author in Colorado named John Eldredge. Eldredge writes books about the masculine journey and I'm a fan of his work. I don't know if it was because David had worked for John or whether he was just wired differently, but what I liked about David is he had no interest in small talk. David understood life as a journey of the heart and wanted to know how my heart was doing on the journey. To be honest, sometimes I found conversations with him to be tiring. But I realized I only got tired because I was trying to hide. I'd rather talk about football or the weather than my heart. Eventually, I gave in and started opening up to the guy.

We didn't become the best of friends, but he was my best friend. By best friend I mean he was the best person for me to talk to. Every time I walked away from a beer or a lunch with him I was, somehow, a more centered person. He never let me control the conversation with distractions. He'd just laugh them off and repeat the question I was running from.

David and his wife had just had twins, and he was looking for an office outside his home. I knew if I was going to get my life together, I had to do more David time. So I rented an office across the street from his condo, bought him a desk, and let him use it for free. I knew I needed more time with the people I wanted to become like if I was going to change. I decided to get a bit more aggressive about it.

THERE ARE PRUNING SEASONS IN LIFE AND THERE are growing seasons. When I look back on my life, I can tell the greatest growth comes right after you get cut back. David had this sincere and kind way of cutting me back. I don't think he meant to do it, but the guy was like a mirror, always reflecting back to me the truth of who I was. I doubt I would have been capable of a healthy relationship without him.

Before learning to get serious in a romantic relationship, I used women for validation. I'd move from girl to girl feeling too much too soon then finally feeling nothing at all. It didn't take David long to notice the pattern.

In the mornings, before we started working, I'd listen to his stories about feeding the twins in the middle of the night and then he'd listen to mine about my most recent love interest. Pretty soon he confronted me.

We were having lunch at an Indian restaurant and I was telling him about a girl I'd met in Michigan. But rather than asking questions about her, which he normally did, he asked if I was getting my identity from manipulating these girls. He said it seemed strange to act so quickly on a crush.

I was taken aback and defensive. "I don't think I'm being manipulative. I may really like this girl."

He said, "Maybe, but most men don't feel so strongly about this many girls a year, Don. Just last month you were talking like this about somebody else. I think you might be using these girls to numb your wounds. You're addicted to some romantic fantasy, but you can't face the reality that love demands we make a choice and stick with it."

Numb my own wounds? David wasn't being unkind, he was being direct. But it hurt all the same. What hurt most is he didn't see me as strong or masculine for reeling these girls in. He saw me as weak. He saw me as needy.

And he was right.

In every relationship I'd been in I'd fantasized about other women. One woman was never enough. I wanted them all. Some of that was sexual fantasy, of course, but plenty of it was romantic, the kind of daydreams where I'd sweep a girl off her feet and buy her a house and have some kids.

I'd meet a girl, get a little crush going, then start daydreaming about being her hero. This is terribly embarrassing to admit, but I swear there was a camera in my brain always shooting an imaginary television show and I'd cast myself as the fun-loving lead. My costars were interchangeable, sometimes a woman I ran into at a coffee shop, maybe a girl I met at a book signing, but, sadly, none of them mattered much to me in real life. I only used them as bit parts in a fantasy. I never knew what I was doing at the time, or I didn't fully have a conscience about it. I realize this is awful now. I'd be brokenhearted if one of my sons followed in my footsteps.

TALKING EVERY MORNING WITH DAVID HELPED ME realize the girls I'd crushed on were all the same: they were the girls who weren't interested in me in high school. What I was doing was going back and rewriting the broken stories I'd lived in my formative years, trying to fix my broken past. I grew up poor, so most of the girls I fell for later in life were from prominent families. I was never athletic or cool, so the girls I fell for had usually been popular or cheerleaders. I'd never know that stuff until we started dating but something in me sensed it and pursued them as though they were medicine. It's as though my broken identity was trying to validate myself with a certain class of people.

The healthier I get, the more surprised I am at the deceptive desires we so often mistake for love.

Of course, none of this ever worked. My broken identity turned me into a manipulator and my romantic life looked like one of those fishing shows on television, a game of catch and release in which I only held the girl long enough to snap a picture.

ONE MORNING DAVID MENTIONED I SHOULD STOP dating for a season. When he said it I had a quiet panic attack at my desk. I doubt he noticed. I sort of moved my mouse around and stared at the bulletin board behind my desk, imagining David, his hot wife, and their twin daughters waving at me through the window of a space station, all of them rooting wildly for crazy uncle Don, floating around in the cold wearing the puffy white suit of singleness.

"It might be good for you to go through withdrawal," he said. "To detox from all the drama."

Detox? I'm an addict now? I thought.

I fantasized about throwing my stapler at him.

IN THE END, THOUGH, I TOOK DAVID'S ADVICE. I decided to go six months without dating. I'd be lying if I said it was easy. I was at a book signing a few weeks later and met a cute socialite whose uncle was a senator. She stood there and tilted her head and told me how much we had in common through lips as shiny as a crack pipe. It was all I could do to stop shaking her hand. I stared at the back of her head as she walked out the door and hoped we'd mysteriously find each other again after I got out of David prison.

That night in my hotel room I daydreamed about the girl, whatever her name was. In the span of thirty minutes we got married and had some kids and one day when we were in our sixties her uncle and I sat in my posh library drinking scotch when he invited me to run for his seat in the senate. Brilliant.

I hated David so much. He was ruining everything.

But at the same time I could feel the silliness of it all. Most of my romantic accomplishments had taken place in my head. And in those stories there was no risk and so no thrill, just the comfort of sugar.

There was also no character arc. Change only comes when we face the difficulty of reality head-on. Fantasy changes nothing, which is why, once we're done fantasizing, it feels like a bankrupt story.

I ENDED UP TAKING MORE THAN SIX MONTHS OFF. It was nearly a year before I started dating again. In a way, the detox worked. After a few months I had the power to walk away from temptation. But it wasn't until I started dating Betsy that I'd realize how much my fantasy life had negatively affected my relationships.

Here's what happened. I moved to DC to pursue Betsy and, of course, had begun to direct a complete love story in my mind. Betsy would play the beautiful, sophisticated girl who saw me as a hero and I'd play the lovable but hardworking power broker.

In the past, as soon as the girl didn't seem to fit the part I'd imagined for her, I'd start focusing on how complicated the relationship was and move on to some other short-lived fantasy.

Betsy wasn't who I thought she would be. She came from a great family and had worked around congressmen and senators on the Hill but had little desire to marry one. She saw them as too busy and in a constant struggle to provide emotional support for their families. And more than anything else, she wanted a healthy family. Her relationships were more about shared memories and common values than about strategic partnerships to help each other succeed. That one killed me. I'd ask why we were getting together with so-and-so and she'd say something about how they hadn't seen each other in a long time and one time they'd stayed up all night smoking cigarettes on the lawn and talking about boys.

I had no mental category for that kind of friendship. I wasn't sure how that kind of friendship profited anybody anything. What were they trying to build? Who were they trying to beat? What were the rules of the game, and how were they going to win? These are the questions in life that matter, right?

"Staying up all night smoking cigarettes and talking about boys seems to me a waste of time," I said sweetly.

Betsy rolled her eyes.

"Sometimes the real bonding happens in conversations about nothing, Don," she said. "Sometimes being willing to talk about nothing shows how much we want to be with each other. And that's a powerful thing."

She might be right. I'm unwilling to say at this point. God knows I'm not staying up all night to sit on a lawn and talk about nothing. Betsy said if we have children I'll do it and I suppose I will. It's funny what happens to you when part of your heart gets born inside somebody else. I trust I'll do the crazy things parents do and they won't seem crazy.

I once took the DISC test, a test that assesses your work style and offers a report people can read if they want to know how to work with you. My report said, "Never talk to Don about anything that doesn't advance his goals." It might as well have said, "Don is a monster. Do not look him in the eye."

BUT THERE WAS SOMETHING QUITE BEAUTIFUL about this new thing with Betsy. She was taking me somewhere. I'd known enough older guys who gave their lives to their careers and have nothing to show for it save a lot of money and power and loneliness to realize Betsy was right. Relationships matter. They matter as much as exercise and nutrition. And not all relationships help us reach our goals. God doesn't give us crying, pooping children because he wants to advance our careers. He gives them to us for the same reason he confused language at the Tower of Babel, to create chaos and deter us from investing too much energy in the gluttonous idols of self-absorption.

So this time I had to stay. I couldn't run from Betsy like I had all the other girls. I had to face the reality I would never be the director of my own distorted love story. I had to realize Betsy would never be an actress reading from a script I'd written. She was herself with her own desires and wants and passions, and there was nothing I could do to control her.

I HAVE A PASTOR FRIEND WHO SAYS THE ROOT OF sin is the desire for control. I think there's some truth to that. And I'd add the root of control is fear. The reason I had such a rich fantasy life was partially because it gave me a sense of control. There was no risk in my fantasy life, and risk is what I feared the most. After all, to love somebody is to give them the power to hurt you, and nobody can hurt you if you're the only one writing the script. But it doesn't work. Controlling people are the loneliest people in the world.

Some people play out their controlling tendencies through intimidation or bullying. I've done that, for sure. But it's the same tendency that drove my fantasy life: it's the desire to be the writer of somebody else's script and control all aspects of the story. It's sad. Not even God controls people's stories and he's the only one who actually can.

THERE WAS A TIME WHEN MY CONTROLLING TEN-dencies nearly derailed my relationship with Betsy. It was our darkest season.

Here's what happened: Betsy and I had gotten engaged in DC and were planning to move to Nashville after having the wedding in New Orleans, where her family lives. We started talking about buying a house, and because I knew Nashville better than she did, I narrowed the neighborhoods to the ones I wanted to live in. Without asking for Betsy's input I met with a real-estate agent and had him put us on an automated list, careful to include only options I'd preapproved. Then I started building my railroad. By that I mean I laid long, steel, unmovable tracks to our future that she would never be able to undo. I was going to get the house I wanted and she was going to live in it.

It all fell apart, of course, when Betsy and I traveled to Nashville to look at houses in person. There were whole sections of the map I wouldn't drive into. I did everything but make up stories about nuclear waste dumps and EPA protected habitats for rare birds.

"A double murder happened in that house," I'd say.

"It's brand-new construction," Betsy would protest. "Nobody's had time to get murdered in it!"

The truth is, though, I'd found the house. It was a decently large house a few miles from my office. It had a good yard and a giant field behind it for the dog. There were two separate garages, and I intended to turn one of them into a home gym. It had a large office that would double as a home library and a living room prewired for a television large enough for a sports arena. The guest rooms were far enough from the master I wouldn't have to interact with Betsy's friends, and it was new construction, which means I'd not spend my life studying YouTube videos about leaky toilets. Perfect.

The real-estate agent took us to lesser homes first, saving the one I wanted for the finale. All the other houses were intentionally flawed, so this one would look the best. I was certain of my strategy.

As we toured the home I kept talking about the little things she might find attractive. Plenty of room for guests. A yard large enough for a garden. Old trees. A porch we could eat dinner on while holding hands. She walked through the house quietly, peeking in all the closets. She didn't linger the way somebody does when they're having a moment. I got concerned. I motioned to our agent to give us a little space. He stepped out into the backyard and Betsy and I stood in the kitchen.

"I don't love it," she said.

"You're crazy," I replied.

"I'm not crazy. I think we should go back through our list. This isn't it."

"This is it," I said. "This is exactly it. It has everything you want, Betsy, a sink in the kitchen and everything."

"You haven't even asked what I want," she said straightly.

"What in God's name could you want that this house doesn't have? Do you want a helipad? A water-slide? What's wrong with you?"

There was a look in Betsy's eyes I hadn't seen before. She stood there quietly with her hand on the kitchen counter. The look wasn't anger, exactly. It was more like sadness mixed with fear. It was the look of a trapped animal wondering what its captor was going to do and whether living in a cage might be worse than dying.

"I want you to tell me what's wrong with this house," I demanded. At that point I'd lost the ability to empathize. The thing that was supposed to happen wasn't happening and I felt like my plan was being taken from me.

"I don't know what's wrong with the house, Don. I'm not sure." Her hand was trembling on the counter. She hid it in the pocket of her fleece.

"You're being a bully," she said softly.

"A bully," I said deliberately, as though to accuse her of drama.

There are times in a man's life when he says things he will never be able take back. It's true words can have a physical impact on somebody. A person can concuss with their words. Words can snap as fast as a trap in the woods and leave a victim to writhe for weeks.

"When you have the money for a down payment, or for that matter a mortgage, your opinion will matter a little more," I said.

Betsy's eyes filled with tears. She turned and walked out the door.

IT WAS A LONG TIME BEFORE SHE COULD FORGIVE me. I assure you I never spoke words like that again. They were unfair and unjust. I offer that story to you as a confession. I was wrong. And besides, the reality for Betsy was she held an esteemed position in a large company in DC. Her career was just getting started, but she didn't need me or my money. Her greatest fear was that choosing me over her career would come at the expense of her freedom and identity. She'd gladly give up her career for a family, but she didn't want to lose her identity. She wanted to be Betsy and she wanted to have her clothes and her things and her home, and she wanted all of that both with and apart from me.

They never tell you when you get born a control freak it will cost you a healthy love life. But it's true. You can't control somebody and have intimacy with them at the same time. They may stay because they fear you, but true love casts out fear.

Betsy and I wouldn't feel close again until we'd left DC and moved to New Orleans to prepare for the wedding. And it took many conversations to understand the damage I'd done. Finding her in the woods and prying the trap open was careful work. It took time. Incredibly, she didn't make me pay for my mistake. She didn't play the victim and that gave me the space for self-reflection.

For me, giving up control involved a period of grieving. It reminded me of the difference between writing a book and writing a movie. When you write a book you control every word, but with a movie you share agency with the producer and cinematographer and even the actors. Everybody who touches the screenplay interprets it differently and by the time it makes it to theaters it looks nothing like you imagined. Yet in so many ways, it looks better. The director was able to smooth out your blind spots and the actors gave your characters new dimensions that made them real and beautiful.

The struggle in my relationship with Betsy was all about sharing agency. Was I willing to go into this thing having no idea what the finished product would look like? Could I give up my dream to merge it with hers and settle and perhaps be surprised by what could happen in a shared life?

Betsy and I found a house that worked for us. The garage wasn't big enough to turn into a home gym and the office was smaller than I wanted, but the guest rooms were far enough from the master to ensure privacy from our guests. And we both wanted lots of guests. The place was wired for a giant television, too, a little bigger than Betsy is happy with but, you know, we all make sacrifices. Betsy loves the backyard, though. There's enough room for a garden. She wants to learn to cook food we grow in our own yard. I found a place near town that sells railroad ties and I've been watching YouTube videos about how to make a raised vegetable bed. And you wouldn't believe it, but that same company she worked with in DC hired her to work on a project-by-project basis from home. So she's started her own company consulting with her old associates.

We both have our independence and freedom, but we have those things with each other. It's a paradox, but it works. It all reminded me of what my friend Henry Cloud told me, that when two people are entirely and completely separate they are finally compatible to be one. Nobody's self-worth lives inside of another person. Intimacy means we are independently together.

I DON'T KNOW WHY LOVING A WOMAN IS SCARIER than climbing a mountain or sailing an ocean, but it is. A mountain can hurt your body and an ocean can drown you, but in the end you're still a man for conquering them. Dead or alive, you're still a man. A woman, though, can rob your manhood and reduce you to a boy at the drop of a word. It's no wonder we all try to control each other. Sometimes relationships feel like we're trying to emotionally cuddle with each other at the same time we're tearing each other down.

But love doesn't control, and I suppose that's why it's the ultimate risk. In the end, we have to hope the person we're giving our heart to won't break it, and be willing to forgive them when they do, even as they will forgive us.

Real love stories don't have dictators, they have participants. Love is an ever-changing, complicated, choose-your-own adventure narrative that offers the world but guarantees nothing. When you climb a mountain or sail an ocean, you're rewarded for staying in control.

Perhaps that's another reason true intimacy is so frightening. It's the one thing we all want, and must give up control to get.

9

Five Kinds of
Manipulators

DURING MY BREAK FROM DATING I READ A FEW
books about manipulative people. The best ones were
Henry Cloud and John Townsend's *Safe People* and
Harriet Braiker's *Who's Pulling Your Strings?* Both
books come to the same conclusion: you will never have
a healthy relationship with a deceptive or manipulative
person.

I read these books because another thing I realized

while Betsy and I were dating is that a healthy person in a relationship with an unhealthy person still makes an unhealthy relationship. Those of us who haven't given up quick tricks and settled into the hard, vulnerable work of connecting are likely to struggle.

I was getting my stuff together, to be sure. I wasn't completely healthy yet, but I was healthy enough to begin looking for a different kind of partner. I wanted somebody who could be true, gracious, committed, and forgiving.

Reading Cloud and Townsend, along with Harriet Braiker, let me know what the dominant enemy of any relationship is. It's dishonesty, and specifically the dishonesty involved in being a manipulative person.

Back when I was terrible in relationships I never called it manipulation. A weasel doesn't know he's a weasel, he just does what works to get food. Getting healthy, then, is like becoming human after having spent years as a weasel.

I remember starting to do business with a guy about the time I read those books about safe people, and I had to ask him about some things in his past that seemed shady. He was accused of taking some money from a previous employer. He was honest with me, at first, admitting to all he'd been caught doing. He also promised he'd changed. He kept using the word integrity as though he were trying to rebrand himself.

When I asked why he'd done what he'd done in the first place, what issues caused him to be so deceptive, he didn't have an answer. He just rambled and kept using the word integrity. The whole thing struck me wrong. The soul isn't that much different than the physical body in that when we have a problem, we can diagnose it and a doctor can help us make it better if we change the way we're living. I could have been judging the guy unfairly, but all the people I've met who've really changed from unhealthy to healthy have a story, a story about hitting bottom, realizing what they were doing wrong, and radically changing the way they live so they don't repeat their mistakes. This guy kept giving me a lot of theater about how he'd changed but didn't have a story. Characters only change when they live through a story. I decided to not do business with him.

Former addicts can smell out insincerity in somebody else's story. I'm not judging insincerity, because it could be part of the path to sincerity. Who knows? I'm only saying I don't mistake it for health anymore. It's just drama.

Like I said before, whenever there's lots of drama there's often manipulation. Just last week I watched a news anchor interview the president, and it was astounding. It was as though the interviewer didn't care about the truth or discovering anything. He just wanted to create drama. He kept trying to trap the president, and the president kept giving him safe answers. In the end, I don't think the American people learned anything about the president or the issues being discussed or anything else. We'd just been entertained for a half hour by two guys wrestling over words.

MANIPULATION MAY BE ENTERTAINING, AND IT MAY help us control people and compel them, but it has a downside in relationships.

I had a humbling conversation with Betsy not long ago. She pointed out that often, when I got off work, I gave her a more glowing report of how the day went than what was technically true. I have a large side business helping brands tell their story, so I'd talk about how we had worked with a major new client . . . and then an hour later explain it was only an introductory phone call. I could hardly help it, though. I wanted her to know how excited I was and how great we were doing. But Betsy said I'd done it a few times and lately she'd found herself not getting excited until she understood the "whole truth." Ouch. After that, I started underselling and overdelivering on news about the new business. She was always delighted to find out things were going better than I'd let on. It helped her trust me more.

ONE OF THE THINGS HENRY CLOUD AND JOHN Townsend convinced me of in *Safe People* is that deception in any form kills intimacy. Because intimacy is based on trust, any form of manipulation will eventually break that trust. Manipulation, then, became the enemy. Betsy and I would spot it watching television, mostly news channels. We noticed newscasts stirred up fear about what might happen, shame toward anybody who disagreed with the host, and intimidation by the host to get the guest to comply. It was too much.

In fact, the whole thing kind of turned into a game. We came up with five categories of manipulation and, in a light way, of course, we'd point out whenever one or the other of us was being manipulative. It's insanely difficult to stop doing it. It's like manipulation is a default mechanism of being human. Sometimes, in more serious conversations, we used the five kinds of manipulators to correct each other. We didn't want manipulation to be part of our relationship.

HERE ARE THE FIVE CATEGORIES OF MANIPULATION Betsy and I identified. We're both guilty of all of them, but we work to keep them in check.

 The <u>Scorekeeper</u>

WHENEVER SOMEBODY STARTS <u>KEEPING SCORE</u> IN <u>a relationship</u> the relationship begins to die. A scorekeeper makes life feel like a contest, only there's no way to win. Scorekeepers are in control of the scoreboard and frame it any way they want, but always in such a way they're winning.

I agree with Harriet Braiker when she says manipulators see the world as a zero-sum game. What she means is a manipulator doesn't believe there are any win-win situations. If somebody else wins, that means they lose, and they have no intention of losing. Scorekeepers keep tabs on whatever favors you owe them and call in those favors when they want to control you. Scorekeepers will call in their favors by saying you don't owe them anything, as in, "You don't owe me for that time I dropped you off at the airport, but I'm traveling next week and . . ."

As a writer, I hear the line, "I bought copies of your books for all my friends, so could you come over for my next book group . . ." all the time. If they wouldn't have phrased the request like a barter I might have gone, but

I know if I give in to a scorekeeper I'm entering the twilight zone where I'll have to submit to the rules of some made-up game. In true, intimate relationships, people don't keep score.

The Judge

I REMEMBER BEING AT DINNER WITH A FRIEND many years ago. I'd not met her family yet and we were only getting to know each other. No more than half an hour into dinner, she said something peculiar. She said, "There may come a day when you meet my mother. I just want you to know, I think she's right about most things. And I'd hate for you to disagree with her."

I said, "I'm sure she's a wise woman and really great, and who knows whether we will agree about things or not? Time will tell."

At that point she began to cry. She wiped her eyes and said, "You don't understand, I don't want you to disagree with her."

Later, when I met her mother, I realized she controlled people by judging them. From an early age my friend learned her security, her food, her shelter, and even the love she received depended on one thing: Mom is always right. And she simply couldn't get close to anybody who threatened that security.

A Judge personality strongly believes in right and wrong, which is great, but they also believe they are the ones who decide right and wrong and lord it over others to maintain authority and power. Right and wrong are less a moral code than they are a collar and leash they attach to others so they can lead them around.

When a Judge personality is religious, they'll use the Bible to gain control of others. The Bible becomes a book of rules they use to prove they are right rather than a book that introduces people to God.

Normal, healthy people don't like being wrong, but they're willing to admit it when they are. Those who manipulate by playing the role of Judge have a problem explaining any kind of specific wrong they've ever committed. The truth is, they don't believe they are wrong at all. To be wrong is to give up control, and manipulators don't give up control.

The reality is, though, you can't have a true, intimate relationship with people you control. Control is about fear. Intimacy is about risk.

The False Hero

THE FALSE HERO MANIPULATES BY LEADING people to believe they have something better to offer than they do. This one's tough because this is my go-to form of manipulation.

I know of at least three girls I dated with whom I talked about marriage and kids well before I was sure they were the one I wanted to marry. Playing the False Hero was my way of gaining security before real security could be established, and I did it at the expense of others.

When Betsy and I started to get serious, I explained this is one of the ways I manipulate. Of course there's a good side to the False Hero personality. I love talking about the future. I love dreaming and building and heading toward a specific place on the horizon. But the dark side to the visionary personality is they can lead people to believe they have a future when it might not be possible, or realistic, to actualize that vision.

You might be dealing with a False Hero when the future they're describing seems too good to be true. If I could go back in time and sit down with some of the employees I had or girls I dated, I'd whisper in their ear to stay away from me.

The Fearmonger

A FEW SUMMERS AGO I VISITED UGANDA AND WHILE there met with members of the judiciary who were piecing together a new constitution and a new democracy. They were still recovering from the reign of a Fearmonger, perhaps the most deadly and dangerous of manipulators. Idi Amin Dada ruled the country for nearly a decade, committing the extrajudiciary extermination of political enemies. It's estimated under Amin's rule between one hundred thousand and five hundred thousand Ugandans were murdered.

Fearmongers rule by making people suffer the consequences of insubordination. The mantra of the Fearmonger is: If you don't submit to me I'll make your life a living hell.

Fearmongers manipulate by making people believe they are strong. They are never vulnerable and fear being perceived as weak. Fearmongers are completely incapable of vulnerability and, as such, incapable of intimacy.

Not long ago I watched a documentary about the current crisis affecting the Catholic Church. Hundreds of priests around the world have been accused and even found guilty of molesting young boys. Many psychologists believe these molestations have little to do with homosexuality and are instead based on a need for certain personality types to dominate others. According to some psychologists, these specific and disturbed priests molest boys to establish their dominance and to get comfort from dominating the weak, even sexually.

You know you're with a Fearmonger when they

overemphasize the concept of loyalty. Certainly loyalty is a virtue, but what a Fearmonger calls loyalty could better be described as complete and total submission. Fearmongers surround themselves only with people who will submit. In exchange for your submission, Fearmongers offer strength and protection, which, for many, is a security they are willing to trade their freedom for. Find a Fearmonger and you'll easily find a team of fearful, submissive personalities doing their will.

I remember when I was a kid our small church brought in a new pastor, a fearful man with a booming voice who loved to preach about God's wrath and the threat of hell. His first sermon was entitled "Appoint Those You Trust and Trust Those You Appoint." It was his way of saying, "Never question or challenge my authority." For the next few years he destroyed our community. He got rid of all the elders and then the entire staff. The lone elder who questioned him was publicly chastised until he committed suicide. In the lobby the new pastor posted lists of tithing and nontithing members so everybody could see who wasn't giving money to the church. His wife was a kept woman and his children were despondent. Eventually, he was asked to leave. He later started an organization that attempted to unite Christians to take over the government. His family was in shambles but nothing could stop him. He continues to wreak havoc today.

When you are afraid to disagree with somebody or challenge their authority, you are likely in the presence of a Fearmonger.

The Flopper

HAVE YOU EVER WATCHED A EUROPEAN SOCCER game in which players dramatically fall down in order to earn a yellow card? Or closer to home, have you watched an NBA game in which a player is hardly touched but slides across the floor as though he was hit by a car? If you have, you've seen a Flopper in action.

A Flopper is somebody who overdramatizes their victimhood in order to gain sympathy and attention.

Floppers assume the role of victim whenever they can. This is a powerful and destructive form of manipulation. In order to be a victim, a person needs an oppressor. If you enter into a relationship with a Flopper, sooner or later that oppressor will be you.

Flopping may sound innocent enough, but it isn't. The people who lose out because of Floppers are legitimate victims. There are people in this world who are taken advantage of every day, and Floppers steal needed resources from them by faking emotional injuries in order to gain control of the people around them. A Flopper's internal mantra goes something like this: If people hurt me they're in my debt, and I can hold it over them to get what I want.

False victims are, themselves, passive oppressors. They seek control by making you feel guilty about what you've done. They don't want to reconcile, they want control. And again, this takes needed attention from people who are truly hurting and helpless.

A true victim is somebody who has no way out and is not in control. A Flopper has plenty of ways out of their circumstances but chooses to stay for the power it brings them. If you consistently feel responsible for somebody else's pain, but you can't figure out how you caused it, you're likely in a relationship with a Flopper.

I'D BE LYING IF I LED YOU TO BELIEVE I WAS ONCE a manipulator and I snapped out of it. The reality is I got help. I'd been in so many bad relationships I finally had to face the reality of my own issues.

But it wasn't just getting help at Onsite. It was also people like Betsy and even my friend David.

Both Betsy and David are truth tellers. There isn't an ounce of guile in either. It's intimidating. I've never known either of them to exaggerate, flop, intimidate, or romanticize a circumstance beyond what is real and true.

But here's the other thing they offer, and I think it's what helped me learn to be more true. They offer grace. I'm talking about the kind of grace in which they assume I'm a really great guy who's just trying to figure things out, and they politely show me the error of my ways.

I can count on one hand the number of times I've felt judged by Betsy. She has this magical, strategic way of waiting for the right time to bring up one of my faults. And she always talks about it in such a way I know she wants me to be stronger and better and for us to have a better relationship. I can't explain it, exactly, but it's almost like a coach coaching an athlete. The athlete never feels weak. It's just that the coach is seeing things the athlete is blind to. The coach is making the athlete stronger.

In this environment of grace, with both Betsy and David, I could finally begin to change.

I say all that because the list I just gave you is dangerous. The old me would have taken that list and used it like ammo at a shooting range. I'd have been shooting manipulators out of the sky, scorekeeping over their faults, which would have made me even more of a manipulator myself.

These days, when I spot a manipulator, I don't feel much judgment at all. If they want to do business together I keep my distance, but that doesn't stop me from liking them. And if we happen to be close enough, and I've earned their trust, and they seem like they want to figure themselves out, I've occasionally said something. But I say it like a coach talking to an athlete, with full respect and admiration. It's a hard thing to be human. It's a very hard thing. Nobody needs a judge or a scorekeeper lording their faults over them.

IN THE BOOK *SAFE PEOPLE*, HENRY CLOUD AND John Townsend define what a safe person is. They say it's somebody who speaks the truth in grace. I like that. And the only hope a manipulator like me had to become a safe person was to surround myself with safe people.

10

Lucy in the Kitchen

BETSY AND I WENT TO LA LAST MONTH TO VISIT MY
friends Marshall and Jamie. They're our second set of
friends who've recently had twins. The kids were born
early so they had to spend an extra month in the hospital. They didn't weigh much more than helium balloons
so the nurses kept watch on them to make sure their
lungs developed. "It happens all the time with twins,"
Marshall said. "They are still developing, but all signs
are good." I had a cough that day so I couldn't see the
babies. Betsy scrubbed her hands in a giant sink and

practically had to put on a rubber suit just to hold them. When she came out she said they were as tiny and pink as hamsters and oh so fragile. She said their little mouths would open wide enough for a scream but their voices came through wispy and quiet.

They were tired, Marsh and Jamie. They're both actors on television shows but had taken the season off to live near the hospital. We walked to a local taco shop together and even a quarter mile from their new babies their hearts were being pulled back to the hospital. They had that weary look like they wanted to go back lie on a bed with their babies, and dream to the sound of their breathing.

WE ATE TACOS BECAUSE PARENTS HAVE TO EAT. We talked about the stages of life and Jamie apologized for looking tired and joked with Betsy that this is where her life was headed, toward tacos and sweatpants and breast pumps and sleepless nights. She said all the beauty of falling in love and posturing and flowers and walks on the beach was a path headed toward worried prayers and sleeping in the car outside a hospital until visiting hours commence. Even as she said this she smiled, as though sacrifice is what makes a story beautiful. Hard but beautiful.

We had the usual conversation about what it's like to become parents and how our perceptions of life change and so on, and then Jamie said something I'd never heard a parent say before. She said, "You know, Don, I've become protective of what people say to my children. It's surprising how many people already want to name them."

I told her I didn't know what she meant and so she explained.

"They'll pick up my son and say something like, 'Oh, look at you, you're going to be a little rebel. You're going to make trouble for everybody, aren't you? You're going to be a firecracker.'"

"Okay," I said, having heard a thousand people say that stuff to a thousand babies.

Jamie said it infuriated her, though. "Nobody is going to label my kids," she said. "They're not even out of the hospital, for crying out loud." Jamie said as soon as somebody does that she politely takes the baby back and when the person leaves the room she whispers to the kid not to listen to them, that they can grow up and be whoever they want and nobody gets to tell them who they are except God.

Marshall agreed. He said before they had the twins he thought of himself as a provider and protector, as somebody who was responsible to protect the physical world around the people he loved. But after having kids he realized that was 10 percent of the battle. What he really had to protect was the twins' identity. He said there was a primal thing in him that wanted to stand between his children and the world and fight back all the lies.

THE WHOLE THING REMINDED ME OF A LESSON I learned from my dog, Lucy. She's a chocolate lab with a timid heart.

In fact, when I got her I'd just read the book *Marley and Me*, and in that book John Grogan is told that when he goes to pick his dog from the litter he should yell boo to see which dogs are timid and which are brave. John's father said he should choose the dog that is the bravest because that's the alpha dog, the pack leader. John did just that and ended up with Marley, who while lovable also ate all the furniture and dug up half the backyard. At one point John follows Marley around sifting through his poop to try to find a piece of his wife's jewelry.

After reading the book, I decided to do the opposite. Lucy's mom lived in a log cabin in the Columbia River Gorge right at the foot of a waterfall. I sat down next to the litter and rubbed her mama's ears. The puppies came toward me, pawing at my legs and biting on my shoestrings. I let out a boo and the litter scattered, but none of them scattered faster than Lucy. She turned and looked at me and peed herself. "That's my dog," I said to the family who owned the cabin.

I've never regretted it. You don't have to even discipline Lucy. You can have a mildly disappointed thought about her and she senses it and whimpers up to your ankles as though to apologize. I can count on one hand the times I've even had to use a leash.

I only tell you this because a few years ago I let a friend stay in my house for a weekend while I was traveling. She had some friends over for a party and I think one of them did something to Lucy.

I didn't realize it for a few days, but one night when I was making dinner I realized Lucy wasn't around. She normally lies on the kitchen floor waiting for a scrap of food to fall, but she wasn't in her usual spot. I checked the living room and she wasn't there, and she wasn't in the dining room either. Finally I found her in the bedroom, hiding half under pillows, shaking. I sat down next to her wondering what had frightened her, but nothing seemed obvious. After an hour or so she returned to normal until the next night when I was making dinner and she did it again. After a while I realized that whenever she heard a pan being pulled from the drawer under the stove she ran into the bedroom and hid. Each night I'd go and sit next to her and rub her ears and talk softly to her, but the damage had been done.

I'm not sure what happened, but what likely explains it is that one of my friend's friends decided to teach Lucy to stay out of the kitchen. Probably some party trick he learned about dogs, that if you scare them you can get them to do what you want.

But it bothered me. I didn't like the fact somebody had trained my dog, somebody had gotten to her. I didn't like the fact that every night she had to experience terror over nothing.

I know Lucy's just a dog, but the experience caused me to wonder how many people have been made to fear something because somebody else had an agenda.

With a dog, it's pretty simple. You can just scare them and they run and hide. With people, though, it's more complicated. The way manipulative people train others is by attacking their identity. They clang the pots and pans of lies about who they are, how terrible they are, and send their victims running into the bedroom, shaking.

AS A WRITER I GET THIS KIND OF TREATMENT FROM time to time. Several of my books have been about my faith journey, and when you talk about religion you are definitely walking into somebody's kitchen.

I consider myself a conservative thinker but an open thinker all the same. New ideas don't scare me. Scary ideas don't even scare me. Every few years, an angry theologian will go on a rant against me. It's all a bit silly. And I suspect what they're really trying to do is not just label me, but scare me. If I don't agree with them, I'm going to go to hell. If I don't agree with them, I'm a horrible person. And they're quite scary. One theologian who came after me was actually fired by his seminary over anger-related issues.

Some people fell for it though. They'd show up at a book signing and hand out leaflets saying I was part of a group of thinkers trying to destroy America. The camp grew into websites and blogs and Facebook groups. Suddenly I was being lumped in with liberal theologians I'd never heard of. They were convinced we were all friends, meeting in caves to cook up our conspiracies.

What was sadder than this, though, is I began to doubt who I really was. Was I a bad person? Were my ideas dangerous? Were there only two teams in the world, the good guys and the bad guys, and I was playing for the bad guys?

More than just feeling like a bad person, the labeling made it harder for me to connect with people. I'd meet somebody and wonder whether the look in their eye meant they thought I was a bad person. About a year or more of that and I just wanted to stay away. I'd become like Lucy, running off to the bedroom. All the scare tactics were working. I was being driven out of community. Like I said earlier, when we don't believe we are good or lovable, we isolate.

I'VE A FRIEND WHO WAS ATTACKED FOR MORE THAN a month by a well-known cable personality. My friend wrote a book encouraging Christians to work toward social justice and the talk-show host labeled him a socialist. He said my friend was one of the enemies of America and essentially made a lot of fearful people think my friend was the Antichrist. The talk-show host talked about him on the show for nearly a month, putting his name on his blackboard of enemies.

Right in the heat of it my friend visited my home and talked about how little of what the talk-show host was saying was true and how much it was affecting his family. Misguided and angry fans of the show were writing him death threats, and his wife feared for their lives. My friend took the high road, though, only responding to the host regarding the issues, quoting the Bible and never making it personal. The talk-show host continued to go after him but he kept turning the other cheek until, finally, the talk-show host let go of it.

And it's not just the conservatives labeling people to stir up drama. Back when I was in DC chasing Betsy, I found myself at a backyard barbecue on Capitol Hill. It was mostly Betsy's friends so I ended up talking to a guy who didn't know many people at the party either. He turned out to be a Democratic political strategist. He makes commercials for senators and gubernatorial candidates, essentially attacking their opponents. You'd think he'd be an arrogant, biting guy but he wasn't. He was thoughtful and tender and even a little sorry about what he did for a living. Certainly he believed there was good in it all, but the more we talked, the more I recognized a sense of conviction about the tactics he employed.

"My job is to scare the hell out of senior citizens in southern Florida and convince them their medical benefits are going to be taken away," he said.

"Is that true?" I asked.

"Not really," he said with a bit of regret in his eyes.

"But that's not the worst part," he continued. "The worst part is what we all do to each other. When a campaign gets to the national level, it gets ruthless. On both sides. You would think these candidates are big enough to take it, but nobody can take it. Every day on a television somewhere, you're being lied about. Your character is being assassinated. People turn and walk away from you at the grocery store. They pull their kids close. I've seen very powerful men reduced to tears. I've seen it happen with my candidates, and I'm sorry to say I've done it to others."

We talked for the better part of two hours. He talked about how when he was young it was almost fun. It was a war. But he's old enough now to see the damage.

The most frightening thing he said to me was this: "Don, you'd be surprised at how easy it is to convince the American people that a perfectly good man is a demon."

I'll add this to the mix too: I believe God is a fan of people connecting and I think the enemy of God is a fan of people breaking off into paranoid tribes. And I think all the clanging pots and pans in the kitchen to scare people from the territory we feel compelled to defend is playing into the hands of dark forces. I think a lot of the shame-based religious and political methodology has more to do with keeping people contained than with setting them free. And I'm no fan of it.

LAST WEEK I WAS WRITING IN A COFFEE SHOP WHEN an old friend walked in. I'd not talked to him in the better part of a year but the rumor mills had been churning. He'd cheated on his wife and was in the middle of a divorce. Worse, the woman he'd cheated with was married, too, so he'd found himself in the trenches between rightfully angry spouses and an army of lawyers.

He came over and I gave him a hug. He sat and asked if I knew. I told him I'd heard stories. He said they were likely true. He said he was sorry. He said he didn't know how things were going to end, didn't know if he was really repentant, didn't know much of anything anymore.

Sometimes our identities get distorted because people lie about us and scare us, and sometimes our identities get distorted because of things we've actually done. The result is the same, though. Isolation. Paranoid tribes.

As my friend told me bits of the story, he described the destruction that happens when you betray a heart. The deeper you fuse your soul to somebody, the more damage you do when you become a bomb. Not many people would talk to him. He understood their anger. He wasn't playing the victim. He seemed like a man who was neither proud nor sorry but certainly confused. Contrite, perhaps, but confused. And who of us hasn't landed there for a season after we screwing up?

I didn't know what to say, but I knew there was

a war happening in his soul, a war for his identity. I knew he would either become Lucy in the bedroom, or some other dog biting the leg of the guy clanging the pans.

I used to get mad at guys who'd made the mistakes my friend has made. Their lives seemed so dark and even evil that I wanted to distance myself from them. I felt that way about those guys until an acquaintance made a similar mistake and was shunned, and right about the time we all forgot about him the news broke about his suicide.

Who was I to judge? When my friend Bob called to encourage me because of the relational mistakes I'd made, he didn't call to condemn. There was plenty of that in my life. But Bob called to be a crack of light in a dark room, something to crawl toward. So I told my friend something like Bob told me.

"I'm not sure of what all you've done," I said to my friend. "And I know some people hate you. But I think you're pretty good at relationships."

My friend looked at me confused. He laughed a little, then sighed, then teared up. "It's true you're bad at relationships," I said, "but it's also true you are good at them. They're both true, old friend." I reminded him of all the people who love him and all the people he's loved. I told him I thought it was unfair for a man to be judged by a moment, by a season. We are all more complicated than that.

Certainly my friend will have to face the consequences of his actions, and those consequences will be severe. He is being pruned, as it were. His limbs are being cut back. But I hope he doesn't live into his failures the way so many people do.

My hope is such a fierce pruning will help create a strong and tender man who understands himself and people and the nature of love better than he ever could have before he made his mistakes. I believe in such miracles.

I DON'T KNOW WHY IT IS, EXACTLY, BUT THE PEOPLE with the healthiest self-esteem are also the greatest at intimacy. I'm not talking about arrogant people. I'm talking about people who know they are both good and bad yet believe at the deepest level they are really good for people.

It's a beautiful moment when somebody wakes up to this reality, when they realize God created them so other people could enjoy them, not just endure them.

I'd say one of the reasons Betsy is good at relationships is, for the most part, she truly believes she's good for people. Again, it's not arrogance. Nobody who knows Betsy would think of her as prideful. Yet she knows that when she gets close to somebody she will likely make their life better. I could count the ways. She's taught me to hold my tongue. She's helped me roll my eyes at drama. She's helped me realize life is more about connecting with people than it is about competing with them. And she's not directly taught me any of this. She doesn't try to change people, she just knows when people spend enough time together, they become like each other. I doubt she even knows how much better she makes the people around her.

One of the best conversations I ever had with Betsy happened when I asked why she thought I was good for her. I'd been wondering about it for a long time but I'd never brought it up. I could count the ways she was good for me, but had no idea why I was good for her.

We were walking Lucy up near the Capitol when I asked. She laughed for a second. "Are you serious?" she asked. "You really don't know?"

"I don't think I know," I said.

I'm glad I finally asked the question. Betsy's answer changed me. She helped me believe I wasn't just good for people, I was great for them. She said I had a way of not getting rattled when things were tense and that brought peace to her life. She said I loved adventure and without me her life wouldn't be half as exciting. She said ever since we'd started dating she'd stopped doubting whether she was beautiful because I told her she was beautiful every day. She went on and on and talked about all the ways I was making her a better person.

Not long after that conversation I found I enjoyed getting together with people a great deal more. Whereas before I'd endure having to get coffee with people, I began to enjoy sharing a bit of our stories. I realized that one of the reasons I'd been so isolated was because I'd subconsciously believed I wasn't all that good for people.

It's true what I'm saying. If our identity gets broken, it affects our ability to connect. And I wonder if we're not all a lot better for each other than we previously thought. I know we're not perfect, but I wonder how many people are withholding the love they could provide because they secretly believe they have fatal flaws.

ALL THIS REMINDS ME OF THAT SCENE IN THE movie *Moneyball* where the general manager of the Oakland A's is struggling with a crisis of identity. Billy Beane and his friend Peter completely rebuilt the team using a model in which they studied statistics rather than using their instincts to decide which players to field. And the system worked. The A's started slow but ended up winning their division, including a record-setting twenty-game winning streak. Billy Beane completely changed the way managers approached the game forever.

In the end, though, the A's didn't win the World Series, and Beane felt like a loser. He believed that unless you were the greatest, you weren't great and he sulked. He was even called in by the Boston Red Sox and offered a twelve-million-dollar contract to manage the team, but that wasn't enough to convince him he was good. Finally, his friend Peter called him into the film room and sat him down.

"I want you to see something, Billy."

"I don't want to watch film," Billy said.

"Just watch this," Peter said and started rolling a clip of a 240-pound infielder for the AA Diamondbacks who was known not only as a power hitter but also for being too slow and too scared to round first base.

In the clip, the young baseball player hits the ball solidly and feels so good about it he decides he's going to try to take second. But tragedy happens. As he rounds first, he trips on the bag and lands on his belly. His worst nightmare had come true. He tried and he failed.

Peter paused the tape and rolled it back and forth so Billy could see how funny the guy looked as he tripped over the base.

"Ah, that's sad," Billy said. "They're all laughing at him."

But Peter let the video roll and asked Billy to keep watching. As the camera closed in on the player crawling on his belly to make sure he was safe at first, the first basemen leaned down, telling him to get up and keep running. The guy looked up in confusion, his helmet nearly covering his eyes. "You hit a home run," the first baseman yelled. "You cleared the back fence by sixty feet."

Billy didn't say anything. He just sat there thinking about the video still rolling on Peter's computer.

You don't even know you hit a home run, Peter implied.

I think about that scene from time to time when I meet with somebody who's been lied about or made a few mistakes, whose identity is under siege.

They don't even know, I think. They don't know they can still live and love and connect. They don't know who they really are and what they're capable of.

They don't know how healing that could be to the people around them. Somebody got to them and shut them down.

11

The Risk of
Being Careful

I SPENT TWENTY YEARS IN PORTLAND BEFORE I moved to DC to pursue Betsy. We'd been friends for years and dated long-distance for six months before I made the decision to chase her.

I never thought I'd leave Portland. I loved that city. There's a spirit of freedom in Portland you can't find many other places. Austin has it a little, and Boulder has it. Nashville is glowing with it. It's not just a hippie thing either. It's something other, a feeling everybody else in the country is being corralled into buying just a few kinds of clothes, a couple of different records and watching the same television shows, while in these rare cities, these bastions of freedom, people have turned off their televisions to realize there are more than binary options for us to choose from. We don't have to be either conservative or liberal or religious or atheist or divided into this or that categories. We can be ourselves, a conglomerate of nuanced beliefs and opinions.

All that to say, Portland was a sad good-bye. I put my stuff in storage, bought a Volkswagen camper van, and headed east during a rare Portland snowstorm. I built a pallet for Lucy on the passenger seat, covered her in a quilt my grandmother had given me, and the two of us set out like John Steinbeck in *Travels with Charley*. The plan was to pass through DC for a year and then relocate to Nashville, hopefully with Betsy at my side.

I had to end up in Nashville because my company was growing and the staff all lived in Nashville, so regardless of what happened, that's where I'd end up.

Truthfully, without the hope of Nashville, I doubt I'd have survived DC.

It's not anything you'd notice at first. It's a beautiful city, for sure. I'll never forget the night Lucy and I pulled into town. We came right down Constitution

Avenue, the Capitol dome glowing like a wedding cake in the distance. The museums slid by Lucy's window like Greek temples and even she was mesmerized by grandness. Marble seems to glow from the inside when it's lit the right way, doesn't it? And having been on the road for weeks, passing through so many small towns and having camped in so many parks, I confess I got sentimental remembering this is where the miracle of America had begun.

It was wonderful to see Betsy, of course. To hear her voice and smell her hair and remember half the feeling of home is usually a person. I met her roommates, who I'd been told approved of me, and their initial questions were soft and easy. I had a job, yes. I wasn't seeing anybody else, nope. I drank whiskey and loved Jesus, yes. I wasn't selling pot out of the van, nope.

That same night Betsy and I drove the van ten streets away where she'd found an apartment I could rent. It was a brownstone divided into three units. They'd installed a kitchen against a brick wall in the living room, turned a closet into a laundry space, and shoved a bed against the wall. It was a dumpy space yet it cost nearly twice my old mortgage. Only a couple of blocks from the Capitol, this was the neighborhood senators rented crash pads in for a place to sleep the few days they spent in DC. There were black SUVs on every other corner, always with the engines running and men in suits looking out through tinted windows. There were cameras on lampposts.

We moved my clothes, blankets, and boxes of books into the apartment, and Betsy and I settled into our DC routine. They were great days, for sure. Betsy called me every morning before she went to work, and when we were done I'd shower and get a writing session in before walking Lucy to Ebenezer's, where I'd get a coffee and Lucy would take a poo in the lawn across from the Security and Exchange Commission. I'd make a show of cleaning it for fear the guys in the SUVs would arrest me.

In the afternoons, after my second writing session, I'd take Lucy to the Potomac where she'd swim after tennis balls I threw off the dock. When Betsy got off work she'd join us. We spent more days than I can remember sitting in camp chairs by the river.

IT WOULD BE ANOTHER MONTH BEFORE I NOTICED it, though. It wasn't Betsy, exactly. It was the whole town. But it affected Betsy and my relationship. People in DC, for reasons I couldn't figure out, were harder to get to know. I first noticed it when I made a joke and the group I was talking to looked at each other to see if it was okay to laugh. One of them kind of chuckled and changed the subject as though to help me save face, even though I didn't want to save face, or need to, for that matter. The whole thing reminded me of having grown up in a legalistic religious environment.

It was more than just jokes. It was as though people only wanted to eat at restaurants that had been approved of, listen to music other people thought was popular, or understandably, express a political opinion that appealed to a broad demographic.

And there was almost no self-expression. There was no art in the subways, no poetry sprawled on buses, no local art more risky than paintings of flowers. And everybody's wardrobe seemed to have been stolen from the Reagan White House.

I'd done a little work in DC a few years before, so I had a friend in town. Over lunch I asked why people in DC were timid to express themselves. My friend had worked in the White House and answered my question by tilting his head toward the window. I turned and saw the Capitol dome towering high across the lawn.

"Think about it, Don," he said. "Every day fifty thousand people climb out of these buildings and crawl into your neighborhood. And every one of them works for somebody who is never allowed to express them-selves. This is a town in which you get ahead by staying on script. You become whoever it is people want you to be or you're out of a job."

Suddenly DC made sense.

FOR BETSY AND ME, THIS WOULD BE A GIVE-AND-take. As I said earlier, if you want to make Betsy mad, criticize people she loves. She's a loyalist and a pit bull for her friends. I was allowed to criticize DC once and then had to temper my language. The ongoing conversation, then, went from a criticism of DC to the roles that vulnerability and self-expression play in relationships.

I tend to connect most easily with two kinds of people, those who are creating something and those who are easily vulnerable. Both trees grow from the same root, I think, and that's the willingness to take risks.

To be fair, many people would say I put too much emphasis on self-expression. Some might say vulnerability is just another characteristic I developed to create an impressive outer ring in my personality. And they'd likely be right. There are times I've overrevealed myself to come off as interesting. It works for me. Especially in books. It's not like people buy these things for the pictures.

Vulnerability has served me well. It's one of the few ways I've been able to connect with others, including readers. I can't tell you how many people have read one of my books and have written letters saying, essentially, *Me too.* They tell me they felt alone in the world until they read my book. And in a very real sense those letters made me feel less alone too. After all, you don't write books in community. All those words they resonated so deeply with were likely written while I was sitting around by myself in my boxer shorts.

But in DC the vulnerability and self-expression stopped working. I always felt two whiskeys in while everybody I talked to was as polished as a news anchor. I kept looking around for cameras.

It's true people can be as vulnerable as they want. There's no right way to be known. But for me, there isn't a political career worth becoming an actor for. As Bill Lokey from Onsite might say, "How else will we connect with people unless we let them know us?"

LAST YEAR I READ AN ARTICLE ABOUT AN AUSTRALIAN nurse named Bronnie Ware, who spent the bulk of her career in palliative care, tending patients with twelve or fewer weeks to live. Not surprisingly most of her patients had joys and regrets. Bronnie said in the last few weeks of their lives, however, they were able to find a higher level of clarity about what mattered most.

Remarkably, the most common regret of the dying was this: they wish they'd had the courage to live a life true to themselves and not the life others expected of them.

As I read about Bronnie's patients I wondered how many opinions I've wanted to share but held back for fear of criticism; what love I've wanted to express but stayed silent for fear of rejection; or the poems and stories I've never released because I didn't think they were good enough for publication.

It's true I've been hurt a few times after revealing myself. There are people who lie in wait for the vulnerable and pounce as a way to feel powerful. But God forgive them. I'm willing to take the occasional blow to find people I connect with. As long as you're willing to turn the other cheek with the mean ones, vulnerability can get you a wealth of friends.

Can you imagine coming to the end of your life, being surrounded by people who loved you, only to realize they never fully knew you? Or having poems you never shared or injustices you said nothing about? Can you imagine realizing, then, it was too late?

How can we be loved if we are always in hiding?

REALIZING I HAD TO RISK BEING KNOWN IN ORDER to love or be loved by Betsy came in a roundabout way.

It came because I confessed to my psychologist friend Bill Lokey I was struggling with writer's block.

The two aren't unrelated. Being afraid to love and being paralyzed at the keyboard both involve a fear of being known, a fear of making mistakes, a fear of being found lacking.

Here's what happened: I wrote my first book in only eight months. It was a terrific experience. I'd smoke a pipe and hike in the mountains of Oregon and dream about the next scene in the book, then that night write page after page of prose I was convinced would win a Pulitzer. Of course it didn't, but I didn't care. I loved writing. I loved the thrill of having words fly off my fingers and creating new worlds.

I enjoyed writing my second book too. I wrote it in eight months as well and the experience was as enjoyable as the first.

While writing my third book, though, the second book became a bestseller. Suddenly, everything changed. People were commenting online about how they loved or hated it and I found the pressure to repeat terrifying.

I'd sit at the keyboard with their criticism in my head and include so many caveats in a chapter that the words no longer had flow. And worse, I'd have people's praise in my head and be terrified I'd never live up to their expectations.

The third book took me more than a year to write and the next book took me two. My fifth book took me nearly four years.

I was in serious trouble. Like I said, it was Bill who helped me figure it out. I told him I'd been having trouble writing and he said he'd noticed my writing had changed.

"What do you mean, changed?" I asked.

"I mean you're being careful now," he said.

"Careful," I repeated out loud. The word sounded suspiciously true.

"Careful," he said. "I mean, I've read a lot of your stuff and what used to be so fun about your writing is you were the guy willing to say things, willing to say what none of us were willing to say. True stuff, all the same, but stuff most of us hide away for fear of being known."

I doubt Bill knew how much his words would serve me, but they did. He was right. I'd achieved a little success and suddenly there was something to lose. And there was an expectation to meet too. It was paralyzing. Suddenly there was a risk to just being myself.

Later that year I happened to read a book by Dr. Neil Fiore that validated Bill's suspicion about being too careful. The book was called *The Now Habit* and was about overcoming procrastination. Dr. Fiore suggested that succeeding in a career is not unlike walking on a tightrope. The more success we achieve, the higher the rope. As we gain something, we have more to lose. Success causes a ravine beneath our careers that grows more deadly, creating a kind of fear of trying. He said the fear of letting people down is one of the primary reasons people procrastinate.

IS THERE ANYTHING MORE TOXIC THAN THE FEAR of being judged? Judgment shuts us down and makes us hide. It keeps us from being ourselves, which keeps us from connecting with other people.

I read an article in the newspaper last month about a man who had only talked with one other person in twenty-seven years. He lived in a tent in the woods in Maine, reading books and listening to an old transistor radio. About once a month he'd sneak into town and break into a restaurant or a retreat center to steal food from the kitchen. He was finally caught stealing cans of beans from a children's camp. He told the police he'd only said one word to another person in three decades, a hiker he came across in the woods ten years before. Other than that, he'd not spoken with another human being in years.

I told my friends about the article and they were jaw-dropped. How in the world do you live completely alone for three decades? The strange thing is, though my friends were dumbfounded, I understood. No part of me wants to become a hermit, but like I said earlier, I honestly get how somebody could live in the woods like that, completely alone, completely free from the risk of other people. It made me wonder if the months I'd spent alone in a cabin, writing, were so peace-filled because, at least for a month, I'd escaped the constant stress of worrying about what other people thought of me.

HAVE YOU EVER MET ANYBODY WHO WAS completely free? Somebody who was willing to say whatever they thought? I'm not talking about a shock-jock looking for attention. I'm talking about somebody who didn't realize people were judgmental, who assumed people would accept them as they are.

I have, and he was fascinating.

Years ago I knew a guy who suffered a head injury as an adult. He seemed normal until you spent more than five minutes talking to him. He walked normally and talked normally, but after the head injury he became uncomfortably blunt. He'd point out if you gained weight, for example—but not in a judgmental way, only because he was curious. "Does your weight affect how it feels to walk long distances? Are you warmer in winter with the extra layer?" I confess there were times I wanted to choke him. And yet I also envied him, not because he was rude, but because he didn't know he was rude. He had no malicious intent, only the odd trait of saying exactly what he thought.

After the injury he began to dress more like an artist. He wore nice scarves and saved his money for a good hat, a full-round brim with a small feather under the band. He wore bright socks and loved long conversations over supper—rich, funny conversations that could easily replace dessert. If there was a lull in the dialogue, he'd point to you and say it was your turn to talk. "Now you say something interesting."

I can't tell you how many dinner conversations I've had since then when I've wanted to point to somebody and tell them to say something interesting. He was quite useful in keeping the conversation moving.

I bring up my friend because part of me wonders if he's the only person I've ever met who will live a life free of regret. It's like Bronnie Ware was saying, if we go to our graves with our feelings still in us, we will die with regrets.

AFTER BILL TOLD ME I WAS BEING TOO CAREFUL, I went back to the old me, the me who felt permission and grace to express his thoughts and feelings. I realized in order to have a career I was going to have to face the fans and the critics. It's a decision we all have to make in our lives, you know, because at some point we all face the risk of being known.

I knew I wouldn't be completely accepted. The risk of being known is also the decision to be criticized by some. There are judges behind every bush. But it didn't matter to me anymore. I couldn't afford to be afraid to write and my soul needed to be known and it couldn't be known in hiding. I was professionally and personally hungry.

So I wrote. I wrote as though God thought my voice mattered. I wrote because I believed a human story was beautiful, no matter how small the human was. I wrote because I didn't make myself, God did. And I wrote like he'd invited me to share my true "self" with the world.

I felt myself becoming a little sturdier on the tight-rope. The ground beneath me began to sink as I wrote, but I kept writing all the same knowing the whole thing was a mirage, that there was no rope and no risk and no death for falling. I wrote blogs about politics, knowing I'd alienate some of my readers. I wrote about leaders I felt were off base, knowing their followers would slam me on their blogs. As a Christian writer, I wrote about not having attended church in more than five years. I wrote my story. I stepped out and let people know who I was, not as a shock-jock, but in the kind of risk it takes to actually connect with people.

OF COURSE, I WAS JUDGED. I WAS CRITICIZED. TO put yourself out there is to be shot at.

But something strange had happened in my healing, something that went along with the reflective work I'd done to become healthy.

I learned to preemptively forgive. Back when I was at Onsite, a staff member explained that people attack out of fear. Life, to many, is a game of "king of the mountain" and when you stand up they are inclined to take you down.

But here's a thing I've noticed. The greatest leaders, the ones who impact the world the most, are somehow able to turn the other cheek. It's as though they believe so solidly in love, so robustly in forgiveness, they have the ability to forgive and even love those who attack them.

And regardless of the critics, the price was worth it. I began to connect with people through blogs and essays like I'd not connected in years. For every person I'd have to turn the other cheek to, there were ten who greeted me with a kiss. It was all worth it.

TO REMIND MYSELF TO NEVER GO BACK TO BEING careful, I made a list of new freedoms.

It looked like this:

I am willing to sound dumb.

I am willing to be wrong.

I am willing to be passionate about something
that isn't perceived as cool.

I am willing to express a theory.

I am willing to admit I'm afraid.

I'm willing to contradict something I've said
before.

I'm willing to have a knee-jerk reaction, even a
wrong one.

I'm willing to apologize.

I'm perfectly willing to be perfectly human.

WHAT HAPPENED NEXT WAS SURPRISING. MY BLOG tripled in traffic and I nearly finished a rough draft of a book in only four months. That's the fastest I'd written a book. The writer's block was gone, and my career wasn't suffering for fear of being true and honest.

The whole experience makes me wonder if the time we spend trying to become somebody people will love isn't wasted because the most powerful, most attractive person we can be is who we already are, an ever-changing being that is becoming and will never arrive, but has opinions about what is seen along the journey.

I'd be lying if I said I'm completely comfortable being myself these days, but I'm getting better. I'm a little more comfortable, I guess, and I'm willing to work a year on a book rather than four. And more importantly, I'm willing to actually turn in what I write rather than throw it away. And that's an improvement. The fans and the critics alike are now contributing to my work rather than shutting it down.

I LIKE WHAT THE DANCER MARTHA GRAHAM ONCE said, that each of us is unique and if we didn't exist something in the world would have been lost. I wonder, then, why we are so quick to conform—and what the world has lost because we have. William Blake said about Jesus that he was "all virtue and acted from impulse, not from rules." If we are to be like him, aren't we to speak and move and do, to act upon the world and take new ground from the forces that work against our unique genius and beauty? What if part of God's message to the world was you? The true and real you?

MY FRIEND JAMIE STAYED WITH BETSY AND ME last night. He stayed for the last two nights, actually. Jamie runs a nonprofit called To Write Love on Her Arms. The .org serves as a voice for the marginalized. It's a clothing line with a heart.

I remember staying up late to hear Jamie speak at a rock concert one night. The band asked him to say something between their songs and Jamie got up in a sweaty, dark room filled with teenagers and told them there was much to live for, there were songs and dreams and hopes yet to be created. He reminded them that each of them had come to the concert with somebody else, they'd likely come with a friend, and together they could cling to a hope that in the toughest time they would be there for each other.

Honestly, I didn't know what to make of it. I wasn't sure whether he was going to pass out flowers or what he was going to do. He just left it at that and walked off the stage.

The kids gathered around him, asking for his autograph, and he uncomfortably signed their shirts and posters.

It's been ten years since I met Jamie. Since then, the brand he started exploded. He's won awards and grants and appeared on every television show you can think of. People love him. And I swear the guy hasn't changed.

He just keeps saying the same thing, softly, as though from some other planet: We need each other. There's no reason to judge. People are more fragile than you could possibly imagine.

I now consider Jamie one of my closest friends. He's the one to call me when I say something unkind online. He reminds me people are hurting and we are supposed to be bigger than the Darwinian games that tempt us. And not only does he call me on my crap, but I call him when I'm hurting.

Anyway, we were sitting out on the back deck and it was cold. Betsy was in the house getting ready for bed. Lucy was chasing a tennis ball that Jamie and I took turns throwing into the yard.

Jamie is a mystery to me, I remember thinking. He doesn't so much tell a story as he is a story. He puts his heart on the front of T-shirts and sells them.

Sometimes, though, Jamie wonders whether what he's doing is worth it. Can something as immeasurable as love, acceptance, grace, tolerance, and forgiveness create a better world? These aren't commodities measured in financial exchanges, after all.

Then, sitting there throwing a tennis ball, it occurred to me Jamie's power is himself. With no fear, he charges his heart at the pointed world as a measure of sacrifice. It has certainly been broken many times. He risks himself by saying how he really feels and standing up to the forces of conformity, most of them dark.

Since meeting Jamie I've heard countless stories from people who were hurting, lonely, confused, and even suicidal who were able to find a toehold in his words. They love him because he accepted them as they were, told them they didn't have to act, and let them know their story contributed to the beauty.

I know you and I may not be wired like Jamie, but you are wired like you and I am wired like me. The more fully we live into ourselves, the more impact we will have. Acting may get us the applause we want, but taking a risk on being ourselves is the only path toward true intimacy. And true intimacy, the exchange of affection between two people who are not lying, is transforming.

I WROTE JAMIE A NOTE THE MORNING HE LEFT. I sat in the kitchen with the house still asleep, knowing I'd be gone before he woke up. I sat at the counter and wondered what to say to my friend. How do you tell somebody that without him, the world would be a darker place? So I prayed and asked for a line.

I wrote it down and stuck it in one of the shoes he left by the front door. It's a true line. It's true of Jamie. But I want it to be true of you too. And for that matter, me. I don't believe we are accidents in the world, and I don't believe we were supposed to be actors either. I think we were supposed to be ourselves and we were meant as a miracle.

Jamie,

Be encouraged. Your heart is writing a poem on the world and it's being turned into a thousand songs.

Much love,

Don

12

Great Parents
Do This Well

THE STUFF IT TAKES TO BE INTIMATE IS AUTHENTIC-
ity, vulnerability, and a belief that other people are
about as good and bad as we are. And I'm learning these
core values contribute to more than just healthy love
stories, they contribute to healthy families, healthy
parenting.

I'll be honest, my greatest fear is Betsy and I will
have kids who don't like me. I married later in life, so

right about the time my Oreo habit catches up with me my children will be in their rebellious period. I have a recurring nightmare one of my sons will tell me what an awful dad I was right before I clutch my chest and keel over.

Betsy hates it when I talk about it, but it's a valid fear, I think. People are supposed to get married early so they can make it through their kids' rebellious stages while they still have the energy. But my kids will be wearing leather and getting their belly buttons pierced while pushing me around in a wheelchair.

I'm tempted to talk Betsy into having cats instead of kids, but she says we've got it in us and we can do this. Betsy thinks we can do anything. She thinks most of my fears are unfounded. I'll try not to say I told you so when the kids tie us to the coffee table and use us as a conversation starter at one of their wild parties.

If I'm comforted by anything, though, I'm comforted by the fact I've a few friends who have really great kids. I'm talking about kids in their teens and twenties who still love and respect their parents. My friends John and Terri MacMurray have three kids who love them. You'd think at least one would go bad. And my friends Paul and Kim Young have six kids, all adults now, and they still come over to the house and bring grandkids and nobody sprays graffiti on anything. My friends Ben and Elaine Pearson's kids make a point to come over for dinner often and they never steal the silverware. I'm seeing it, you know. I'm seeing an outside shot that a healthy family is possible, that our kids might not grow up and use us as human shields in a string of bank robberies.

I'M NOTICING A COMMON CHARACTERISTIC OF healthy families, though. The characteristic is this: kids with parents who are honest about their shortcomings seem to do better in life.

What I mean is parents who aren't trying to be perfect or pretend they're perfect have kids who trust and respect them more. It's as though vulnerability and openness act as the soil that fosters security. And I'd say that's the quality I most often sense in the children of honest, open parents. I sense security.

Sadly, I've noticed the opposite is true too. I've noticed parents who don't admit their faults have children who are troubled and emotionally restless as though they secretly want to be free from their families so they can be themselves.

Of course there's no sure predictor whether or not kids will do okay in life. There are too many variables. But I believe vulnerability in parenting increases the chance a kid will grow up to become healthy and content in life.

If you think about it, parents who are open and honest with their kids create an environment in which children are allowed to be human. And, sadly, parents who hide their flaws unknowingly create an environment where kids feel the need to hide. And feeling the need to hide our true selves from the world is rarely healthy.

Some of the most troubled people I know were raised in fundamentalist environments with parents who felt the need to act more righteous than they were. I don't know if I've ever met a person from a legalistic family who didn't struggle. Environments in which we are encouraged to hide our faults are toxic.

JUST AFTER BETSY AND I GOT ENGAGED, WE started talking about having kids, about how long we'd want to be married before starting a family. She liked talking about it a little more than I did, but it got me thinking all the same. How was I going to be a good father?

One day, when I was throwing a tennis ball into the Potomac for Lucy, I called my friend Paul Young. Paul is the guy who wrote the book *The Shack*. I met him when he was a warehouse manager, selling copies of his book out of the trunk of his car. Since then, he's sold nearly twenty million copies and has become a global literary phenomenon. And yet his personality has changed little. He's just Paul. Humble, honest, brilliant Paul.

The reason I called, though, is Paul has one of the best families I've met. I mentioned him earlier. He and his wife, Kim, have six kids and I don't think I've met a more open and honest family. Their children are strong and independent and, save the everyday human struggles, healthy. In the past, when I've had dinner with them, I was surprised at how freely and openly they talked through whatever problem they were dealing with. It's as though their family was a refuge, a place where everybody could be themselves with no fear of being judged.

"SO YOU'RE GETTING SERIOUS WITH THIS GIRL?" Paul asked me.

"I am," I confirmed. "She's special, Paul. I think this one's going the distance."

"Well, Don. I'm glad for you. It's about time."

I told Paul the reason I'd called. I told him one of the things I feared the most was that I wasn't going to be a good dad.

Paul sighed. He said he saw nothing in me that would lead him to believe I'd not make a good father. But I pressed. I told him I wanted to know the secret. I wanted to know how he'd approached fatherhood, why his kids loved him and Kim.

Paul paused for a moment. "Well," he finally said, "it didn't come easy. We aren't perfect now, but we're better. I'm honored you would want a family like ours."

Paul paused again, and then he opened up. He confirmed that, indeed, the defining characteristic of their family was honesty and vulnerability. "There are no shadows in our family," Paul said. "We don't hide anything. But that's a tough place to get to. It takes work and it's painful."

Paul went on to explain that years before, when most of the kids were young, he'd had an adulterous, emotional affair with another woman. He said it as openly and honestly as a man in a confessional. It had been a tragic mistake and he was self-deceived, but he did it and he paid the price.

I've met a lot of best-selling authors, but very few of them will talk openly about their mistakes. Most authors, especially religious authors, feel the need to leverage their moral authority, real or perceived. But Paul explained his affair was a grueling season for his family, yet it brought something into their lives they'd desperately needed—the truth. Paul said part of the reason he'd had the affair in the first place is because the survival skill of deception had crept into the relationship. Paul and Kim knew if their family was going to survive, and even thrive, people were going to have to start being painfully honest.

Four of Paul and Kim's children were too young to be told what he'd done at the time of the affair. The older kids knew, but Paul waited a few years before telling the younger ones. When the time was right, though, he and two of the older boys took the third son on a hike, to a quiet place and he confessed what he'd done when they were children. He said the process of confession was agonizing. It was a few more years before it was time to tell the youngest, but Kim sat with them as Paul confessed the truth they had not known about their father.

"You know, Don, there's a difference between apologizing and asking forgiveness," he said. "An apology is a statement, as informal as a press release, but asking forgiveness involves giving power to the person you're seeking forgiveness from. I had to give my kids the power to choose whether they wanted intimacy with me, whether they wanted to forgive me. That's a terrifying and clarifying moment."

"Did they forgive you?" I asked, thinking that while painful, authenticity would have some kind of magic power.

"Not all of them, and not right away," he said. "I cried with them and genuinely felt terrible, but each of them had to process it in their own way. Imagine finding out your father had cheated on your mom and the whole time you never knew about it while other members of your family knew the whole story. You'd feel like you'd been living inside a lie. It was shattering."

"How did you guys get to where you are now?" I asked.

"Each of my children, and my wife for that matter, have different stories," Paul said. "My son initially forgave me right away, but years later when his best friend died in an accident, he began to resent me because, in part, he realized there was a dark side to life and he put me into that category. He began to realize the world could be unfair and I had been unfair and unjust too. We had to work through everything all over again. I stood there and asked for forgiveness once more, allowing him to process it in his own way. Forgiveness is a funny thing. It's not cut-and-dried, you know. But over time, he forgave me and we were able to rebuild intimacy."

"And the others?" I asked.

"One daughter is a protector of others and didn't deal with it right away either, and our other daughter took the news the hardest. She was still young and she worried if I'd cheated on her mom, maybe I'd abused her when she was too young to remember. She thought maybe I was some kind of pervert. I can't tell you how painful that was for me. I'd never hurt her. When she brought her fears, I sobbed."

I couldn't believe Paul was telling me all this, but in a way I knew that's what made him special. In fact, that's what made him powerful. He was committed to being completely true about who he was. He owned it. He didn't want to hide from his kids and he didn't want to hide from me. He didn't want to hide from anybody. He wanted to connect.

Paul sighed. "I told her I hadn't hurt her when she was young, but she didn't know whether to believe me. She actually moved out of the house. She moved into my son's house in town. It was Good Friday. My son had to step into a difficult place and act as his sister's advocate for a season and he did a great job working us toward reconciliation. The next day, Saturday, we gathered at their home, and my day was spent answering any and every question she had, asked within the safety of her family. I sat there and answered. It was wrenching. Occasionally I was asked to leave so the family could talk without me in the room," Paul lamented as he remembered the day. You could tell he still hated what he'd done. "I walked around the block in the rain, weeping so hard I couldn't even see the ground, praying and asking God for help," he said.

"She's obviously forgiven you now. You guys are close," I said.

"Yes. But there was a season we weren't. I went home that day and was feeling utterly exhausted and miserable, and my wife and other daughter decided to go for a walk. They had barely gotten out the door when she called to me. I went out to the porch and there was a beautiful rainbow over the neighborhood. A perfect and complete arch from one side of our street to the other. I really believe that was a gift from God, Don, that he was telling me he could be trusted to do his part in restoring what seemed so impossibly broken. A couple of weeks later, my daughter walked through the door again. I'll never forget it. I was sitting on the couch when she walked in, crossed the living room, and crawled into my arms. I held her and we just sat there and rocked and wept. She whispered to me, 'I get it.' God was good to me, Don. I didn't deserve forgiveness. When I asked for forgiveness, I gave my daughter the power and she didn't keep it as a way to hurt me. She gave it back. She forgave me."

Then, Paul remembered a Bible verse from 1 John. He said that John, in summarizing all that he'd learned about God, said this: "God is light, and in him there is no darkness at all."

"When you are with God," Paul said, "there is no

darkness, ho hiding, no pretending. When you are with God, you have the freedom and courage to be yourself."

THERE AREN'T MANY CONVERSATIONS I'VE HAD that have been more freeing than the one I had that day with Paul. It was about more than fathering or the fear of being a father. The conversation was really about freedom, about being free to be human and honest and true, no matter how dark the truth is. It was a conversation about intimacy, not only with a family but with myself and with God.

Still, the whole thing felt frightening. In ways, life really does seem like a game of poker. There's all this acceptance and power and love in the middle of the table, and we're all holding our cards close to our chest trying to win it. It feels like the dumbest thing to do would be to show our cards.

But later that year I met another guy, another great father who seemed to espouse the same truth, that health only happens when we're able to be known. And not only this, he said we had to become the kind of people others felt safe around so they could be known too. He said unless people feel safe around us, intimacy would never happen.

I MET THIS OTHER DAD WHEN I ATTENDED A SMALL retreat on the California coast with a group of writers and thinkers. My roommate happened to be a man named Mark Foreman. Mark's sons, Jon and Tim Foreman, front the band Switchfoot. I'd known Jon for some time but had never met his dad. Jon is one of the wisest people I've met. He stands on stage night after night with thousands of people screaming his name, but when you sit down over breakfast with him he's balanced. He listens more than he talks and his advice is spot-on and seems to come from a thousand years of wisdom. Guys like Jon are a mystery to me. Or at least guys like Jon were . . . before I met Jon's dad.

It was a tiny retreat, so Mark and I shared a small bedroom with two twin beds just off the kitchen. We'd lie in bed each night and talk about what we'd learned that day. Like his son, Mark mostly asked questions and rather than giving advice told stories from his life. I asked him about his kids too. I asked him how he'd raised healthy sons, especially sons who were able to stay balanced after becoming rock stars.

"There's a lot to that, Don," Mark said to me. "I'm proud of my kids and they're exceptional. If I've helped, I'm glad. But I also think they're just exceptional people. They are some of my best friends, truly."

"What do you mean, friends?" I asked. "Like you confide in them?"

"Absolutely," Mark said. "And they confide in me too. We can tell each other anything. Anything at all."

"How'd you manage to build that?" I asked. It's a question I'm learning to ask often, just about anywhere I see a healthy relationship.

"Oh," Mark chuckled. "That wasn't easy. But it was this single decision I made early on: I decided I wouldn't judge my kids. No matter what they told me, I wouldn't judge them. I might have to discipline them, but I wouldn't make them feel like lesser people for their mistakes. And because of that, they learned to trust me with their deepest thoughts."

"Really?" I asked, honestly wondering how true a relationship between fathers and sons could be.

"Oh yes," Mark affirmed. "I can't tell you how many times we were out surfing, just sitting on our boards waiting for a wave, and one of my sons would tell me what was going on in his life and I had to bite my tongue. I had to sit there and look him in the eye and listen and not scream 'What were you thinking?'" Mark started laughing. "Oh heavens. Those boys. But I'd listen and then tell them a story from my life and share whatever wisdom I could and just try to shake it off while surfing in."

"That's brilliant," I said.

"Well, that was when they were older, you know. We'd taught them the basics early. It's not like we didn't discipline them. But the older they got, the more I listened without judgment as they figured out how to apply wisdom to their own lives. And they've turned out well. I'm proud of them. Like I said, they are two of my best friends. We can tell each other anything."

THE IDEA THAT AUTHENTICITY LEADS TO DEEP AND healthy relationships fixated me for a long time. I'm convinced honesty is the soil intimacy grows in. In researching the idea, I put in a call to Bill Lokey.

Bill was helpful. He said half the battle to healing the soul was finding a safe place where people could tell the truth about who they were. He said the best place a person could learn that was within the family structure, even as early as childhood. He sent over an article from the *New York Times* that summarized the findings of a couple of psychologists on this issue.

It turns out Marshall Duke, a psychologist at Emory University, went looking for common themes of healthy families. His wife, Sara, a psychologist who works with children with learning disabilities noticed something about her students: "The ones who know a lot about their families tend to do better when they face challenges."

The article went on to explain that "the more children knew about their family history, the stronger their sense of control over their lives, the higher their self-esteem and the more successfully they believed their families functioned." In fact, the "How much do you know about your family?" scale turned out to be the best single predictor of children's emotional health and happiness.

Dr. Duke went on to explain, however, it wasn't just honesty about a family's troubled narrative that fueled a child's health. It was actually what he called the oscillating family narrative that is the true story about how the family both succeeds and fails and yet stays together regardless. "Dear, let me tell you, we've had ups and downs in our family. We built a family business. Your grandfather was a pillar of the community. Your mother was on the board of the hospital. But we also had setbacks. You had an uncle who was once arrested. We had a house burn down. Your father lost a job. But no matter what happened, we always stuck together as a family."

As I read that article I was given hope. If raising healthy children involves telling the truth about the family narrative, that was something I could do. It would take some practice and a whole lot of courage, but I could do it. I felt a sense of relief. If honesty is the key to intimacy, it means we don't have to be perfect and, moreover, we don't have to pretend to be perfect.

ALL THIS TALK ABOUT BEING TRUE REMINDS ME OF that scene in *The Wizard of Oz* where Dorothy and the boys stumble up to the Wizard, a giant smoke-breathing machine of a thing that controls Oz with a deep, intimidating voice. But Toto the dog discovers a man behind the curtain and reveals the con to everybody. The Wizard of Oz is just a man. He's just a guy pretending to be somebody better than he is. And in a way you have compassion for him. After all, he does have to keep Oz together, and what better way to do it than to establish control by pretending you're all knowing and perfect?

I like the next scene the best, though, the scene where the man honestly tries to help everybody get back home. He's out of the closet, just a man now, but he still has power, real power. He has the power to encourage them and he reminds them of who they really are. He gives the Lion a medal for courage and the Scarecrow a diploma in thinkology. The Tin Man gets a ticking watch to remind him a heart is more than just a beating piece of flesh. None of those connections could have happened if the Wizard had stayed behind the curtain pulling levers. It's true: if we live behind a mask we can impress but we can't connect.

That scene in *The Wizard of Oz* reminds me of what my friend Paul did for his kids. He stepped out from behind the curtain and gave his kids his heart, broken as it was. And so they connected and the family began to heal.

ALL THAT TO SAY I'VE GOT A LITTLE HOPE BREWING now. I'm hoping my kids will grow up being less impressed with me but more connected to me. And I'm hoping my kids will accept me as I am, flaws and all, even as I accept them.

I suppose building a healthy family is possible. Maybe what children really need is simple. Maybe they just need somebody to show them it's okay to be human.

13

The Stuff of a
Meaningful Life

IF BETSY LOSES ME TO ANYTHING IT WILL LIKELY be work. As I alluded to earlier, when I was young I believed the lie nobody would love me unless I succeeded. It's an easy belief to subscribe to growing up in America. And while I have nothing against success and still enjoy pursuing it, the need for success could have easily derailed my chance at true intimacy.

There were many reasons I didn't get married in

my thirties, but one of them is I didn't want to let go of my need to accumulate money, validation, and influence. I believed if I had these things nobody would want to leave me, yet my devotion to the insane schedule made a healthy relationship impossible. In order to be successful, I'd go off to cabins on remote islands in the winter and isolate to write a book. In other words, to get people to love me I'd walk away from people altogether. I was living in an absurdly unhealthy paradox. And while it was getting me famous, it wasn't creating a meaningful life.

A few years ago, though, some of my confusion began to change. It started when I delivered a eulogy for a man who was like a father to me. He'd been a constant source of encouragement since I was a kid, but I didn't realize how impactful he'd been until he was gone. It took his funeral for me to notice the enormous empire he'd been subtly building by daily giving his life away.

His name was David Gentiles and he was a pastor at my church when I was a kid. My mom used to make me go, and I'm glad. Like I told you before, I was a geeky kid, and David was one of the few adults in my life who even noticed me.

In high school, David invited me to a book group at his house. We'd meet early in the morning and study a classic piece of literature. I wanted the group to like me, so during the week I'd read and take notes and come prepared. It was David who first told me I had a knack for words and even invited me to write for the high school newspaper. I doubt I'd have started to write without his encouragement.

David died in a tragic accident. We don't think our fathers will really die, do we? The ones who speak love into our lives have an eternal way about them. Perhaps the love they shared was the God part of them and we intuitively recognize love as the one thing that conquers death. I don't know. Regardless, I hadn't realized how much of a safety net he'd been or how large a space is taken in our souls by those who believe in us unconditionally.

I was living in Portland when I got the news, so I bought a plane ticket immediately. I wanted to get to Austin early to meet with David's daughters and the people he'd been serving as an assistant pastor. David had gotten divorced years before and since then had chosen to live simply. While he'd been sought for influential positions in large churches, he chose instead to minister to a tiny church. In some ways David lived his career in reverse. His talent grew, but every time he had the chance to move up the career ladder he moved down, on purpose. It's something I never understood. The churches he ministered to kept getting smaller and smaller and the positions he took got less and less glamorous.

IN TEXAS, BEING A MINISTER CAN MAKE YOU A rock star. Pastors of large churches get major book deals and have their pictures on billboards and are chosen to counsel presidents and chime in on morning talk shows. And as I flew to Texas I wondered why David never went that route. He was a fantastic communicator, a great writer, and had more charm and personality than most people who rise to fame.

I'd like to say I thought more highly of David for his decision to keep life simple, but I didn't. I wanted the world to know about him, not just me and a few other people who'd grown up in one of his youth groups.

When I arrived in Austin I was invited to meet with the staff at his church as they prepared for his funeral. We talked about his finances and how the church could take care of his daughters and was surprised to find out David died with very little money and few possessions. In fact, he'd been renting a house for the last few years where he had offered people who needed a place to stay a spare bedroom for free. He drove an old truck that wasn't worth much and his possessions would cost more to sell than dispose of.

Again, I wish I could say I admired him for the way he lived but I wanted him to have had a little money and a car that worked and I wanted him to have enjoyed the pleasures of life a man of his talent deserved. I felt like I knew a guy who could hit a home run any time he went to bat but he'd never even tried to play the game. When he was alive, I'd asked him a dozen times to write a book, so he'd start one then get bored and lose interest. Instead, he'd start a recovery program for addicts.

I SPENT THE DAY BEFORE DAVID'S FUNERAL IN A hotel room preparing for the eulogy. I don't know that I've cried that much before or since. As I thought about him, I realized what was gone from the world was a depth of goodness few of us had experienced in a friend. What was gone from the world was a quiet, unassuming man who believed love mattered more than personal glory. And I knew, at least for me, he'd been proven right. Had he been more impressive I'd not have felt half the pain of his passing. It was his love for me that created the chasm and the ache.

It was a struggle to think about David and compare his life to mine. More people knew my name, but far more people knew him. I wondered which was better: to have all the stuff we think will make people love us or to have love itself? David had love.

What was shocking, though, was what happened next. The small church where he pastored couldn't hold the number of people who wanted to attend the service, so they moved David's funeral to a baseball stadium outside town. When I got there, news trucks were parked in the parking lot with tall antennae raised above the gathering crowd. The parking lot was full, so people were parked along the street to get to the stadium. And all this for a man who died as the assistant pastor of a church with no more than one hundred members.

I sat near home plate with David's family and looked out over the crowd. I felt small in that place. I felt small in my accomplishments and I knew, I knew because it was a fact, love had won the day. Thousands of people had been deeply loved by a man who sought no fame and no glory. David didn't try to impress people. He simply loved them.

For me, the sure sign a story is good is how it makes you feel afterward. When an audience sits in the theater to watch the credits roll, the story was good. It's as though nobody wants to get up out of respect for what they just experienced. And if I had to name the emotion I feel sitting there watching the credits roll, it's gratitude. Not just gratitude for the story, but for life itself. A good story makes you thankful to be alive because it reminds you that while sometimes painful, life is indeed beautiful and even magical. David's funeral felt like that. As painful as it was for all of us to say good-bye, there was a feeling of gratitude in the air. And when the service ended, nobody left. We sat and talked and felt thankful, not just for David, but for how beautiful life could be. I say that because I'm starting to wonder if that's not the whole point of life, to be thankful for it and to live in such a way others are thankful for theirs as well.

THE JOURNEY OF LEARNING TO LOVE RATHER THAN trying to impress was affecting more than my relationship with Betsy. It was affecting my career. The paradigm shift was starting to affect my ambitions and the things I wanted to do with my life.

In a way, my life was getting smaller. After David died, and after some of the broken stuff in my identity began to heal, relationships became more important.

I'd spent the previous decade working alone, but after seeing what David built I rented an office and hired a staff. I'd been doing a conference for years, so I put together a team to try to make it grow. Honestly, though, I did it so I could have a group of people to be with. I wanted a community.

My writing career suffered, of course. Writing demands your complete attention. It's hard to run a company and write a book at the same time. But I didn't care. I made less money and lost some influence, but the relationships in the office were beginning to change me. And I wanted more.

One day, while attending a business conference, I realized that while the principles about management efficiency were helpful, they didn't seem quite right to me. I didn't want my team members to be cogs in a wheel. I didn't want to be a cog in a wheel. Certainly we could do business differently.

So I went back to my room and wrote a manifesto. Our company would exist to help its employees' dreams come true, to challenge each other within community in order to better our character, and to do this by serving our clients with excellence. I also wrote about love, about how it wasn't wrong for people working for a business to love one another.

The next morning the ideas terrified me. I wondered if they were too mushy, if the guys would lose respect for me if I told them what I was thinking. I wondered about my own motives, too, whether I was playing the False Hero or attempting to people-please. I knew this, though: I wanted more than just a company. I wanted something different. I wanted to be in it for more than just a profit.

The next evening I showed these core values to the leadership team, who had joined me at the conference. We sat around in the living room of a house we'd rented and I went through them one by one, asking why couldn't we do business differently? We'd have to make money in order for the system to be sustainable, but the business wouldn't exist to make money, it would exist to build a healthy community.

The team sat in silence. I wasn't sure how the core values were playing until someone spoke up and said he thought they were beautiful. Another said this was the job he'd always dreamed about. And another said if word got out, there would be a line of applicants around the block and asked us not to get rid of him if somebody better came along. We laughed.

Once we got back to the office, our graphic artist made a poster of our core values. We believed we had the power to make one another's professional dreams come true. We believed the work we did affected more than just our clients, but each other. We believed in grace over guilt and we believed anybody could become great if they were challenged within the context of a community. Suddenly we were more than a company, we were a new and better culture. Our business had become a fund-raising front for a makeshift family.

The result was predictable, of course. The company grew exponentially. Everybody wanted to be the first person to the office and the last one to leave. We began to realize there was joy in serving each other. We pay our team members well, but the reality is people want to work for more than just money. They want to work to build and sustain a community they love. As we shared our personal dreams with each other, my work was no longer about me reaching my goals, it was about me contributing to a team in which we'd all tied our dreams together.

ABOUT THE TIME DAVID DIED, I READ VIKTOR Frankl's book *Man's Search for Meaning*. Frankl was a Viennese personality theorist alive during the time of Freud. What differentiated them, though, was Freud posited one of the primary desires of man was for pleasure, that he got up every morning and sought a comfortable or enjoyable life. Frankl contended with him, saying what man really wanted was a deep experience of meaning. Man woke up wanting to feel a sense of gratitude for the experience they were having, a sense of purpose and mission and belonging.

Frankl went on to say it wasn't pleasure mankind was

looking for, that men only sought pleasure when they couldn't find meaning. If a man has no sense of meaning, Frankl argued, he will numb himself with pleasure.

His theory was interesting enough on its own, but as it contributed to my own journey toward intimacy, he helped me see that my selfish ambitions—my desire for applause—would never work.

Frankl theorized a sense of meaning was existential, that it was something that passed through us not unlike the recognition of beauty or a feeling of gratitude. And he believed life could be structured in such a way people would experience meaning. His prescription to experience a deep sense of meaning, then, was remarkably pragmatic. He had three recommendations:

1. Have a project to work on, some reason to get out of bed in the morning and preferably something that serves other people.
2. Have a redemptive perspective on life's challenges. That is, when something difficult happens, recognize the ways that difficulty also serves you.
3. Share your life with a person or people who love you unconditionally.

Frankl called this treatment logotherapy, or a therapy of meaning. And surprisingly, it worked. He was put in charge of the mental-health division of the Viennese hospital system because they had lost far too many patients to suicide. When Frankl came aboard, he had more than thirty thousand suicidal patients under his care. The challenge was phenomenal.

Frankl created community groups for the patients and taught counselors to identify projects the patients could contribute to, serious work the world needed that would give them a reason to get out of bed in the morning. Frankl also had the patients circle the difficult experiences they'd had and while allowing them to grieve, also asked them to list benefits that had come from their pain.

The result of the program was transformational. Not one patient committed suicide on Frankl's watch.

I only bring up Viktor Frankl because, without knowing it, David's legacy, along with my relationship with Betsy and the new community I was building through our little company, had been instrumental in helping me experience a deep sense of meaning. I was becoming less and less the isolated writer seeking applause and more and more a team player working on projects within an unconditionally supportive community. I'd taken myself through logotherapy, and it was working.

I began to experience a deep sense of meaning. I didn't have time to be the sad guy studying my belly button. The guys needed me to produce content for customers and to set a vision for where we were going. I couldn't be the self-ish boyfriend either. Betsy had real needs, and if I didn't meet them her life wouldn't be as enjoyable. I was needed.

NOT LONG AGO I WAS READING A PASSAGE IN THE Bible in which Jesus was praying for his disciples. He prayed that they would love each other, as he'd taught them to do. He prayed that they'd embrace a mission to teach other people to create communities that loved each other, as they'd experienced with him. When I read the passage, though, I saw it differently. He wasn't just calling them into a life of sacrifice. He was calling them into a life of meaning, even the kind of meaning that would involve suffering. Suffering for a redemptive reason is hardly suffering, after all.

LOOKING BACK, ALL THIS HELPED ME UNDERSTAND why David had given so much of himself, why his life had declined in earthly validation all the while ascending in the stuff that really matters.

He had been driven by what I was only beginning to experience: a deep sense of meaning.

14

Do Men Do Intimacy Differently?

HERE'S SOMETHING I HEARD RECENTLY: "MEN move toward whatever makes them feel competent." As soon as I heard that I knew it was true. Every man I know migrates toward something that makes him feel powerful and in control. If it's work, he puts in more hours, if it's sports he's constantly at the gym. I only bring this up because few men I know feel competent in intimate relationships, which might be one of the reasons they don't sit around talking about how well they do or don't get along with the people they love.

That said, I don't think men are as bad at intimacy as we might think. It's just that we get pressured to go about intimacy in ways that are traditionally more feminine, specifically we're asked to talk about it and share our feelings. We don't really want to do that. Even writing this book is difficult for me, not because it's a particularly hard book to write, but because I get tired of talking about my feelings all the time. Whenever it's time to sit down and write, I get that same empty pit in my stomach as I do when somebody wants to have a serious conversation about the soul. I can go there sometimes but it's no place I want to live.

The older I get, though, the less I feel bad about this. I realize there's a risk in making generalizations about gender, because God knows every human being is unique but I think it's safe to say most women connect with people in a different way than most men. I think men do intimacy differently and I think that's okay.

Before realizing Betsy and I do intimacy differently I felt bad about the fact I didn't always want to talk about things. Now I realize that's not how I'm wired and I'm not supposed to be particularly good at it. That's not to say I don't sit and talk about my feelings, because I do and it's important because that's one of the ways Betsy connects. It's just that I don't kick myself around about it feeling slightly unnatural.

I know I'm not alone in feeling awkward around the topic of intimacy. Most of the guys I know feel the same. The problem is most men are actually great at intimacy it's just that we've been led to believe we aren't. And I'm convinced the confusion is costing us.

YEARS AGO I WORKED ON A GOVERNMENT TASK force studying fatherhood and healthy families. As we met in DC, I learned one of the main causes of the breakdown of the American family was the Industrial Revolution. When men left their homes and farms to work on assembly lines, they disconnected their sense of worth from the well-being of their wives and children and began to associate it with efficiency and productivity in manufacturing. While the Industrial Revolution served the world in terrific ways, it was also a mild tragedy in our social evolution. Raising healthy children became a woman's job. Food was no longer grown in the backyard, it was bought at a store with money earned from the necessary separation of the father. Within a few generations, then, intimacy in family relationships began to be monopolized by females.

In my opinion, this has created a couple of

generations of men in a crisis of identity. Desperate as we are to find and prove our worth, men can be tempted to view career as a path toward masculinity. Sadly, children can easily become a confusing hindrance in a man's journey to find a sense of masculine power. Yet the men I know who've bought into this way of validating their masculine identity are often unhealthy. They come off as lonely and desperate. I can't tell you how many men I know who are, like I used to be, serial daters, moving from one woman to another, always three or four girls on the line, never giving a thought to choosing, committing, and wholly satisfying one of them for fear of taking their minds off their careers.

But lately I'm seeing exceptions. Maybe it's because my relationship with Betsy has caused me to notice them. But it's true. There are good men in the world.

LAST YEAR I HIRED AN EXECUTIVE COACH NAMED Daniel Harkavy. My company tripled in size in eighteen months, and I needed help navigating the growth. Dan runs an organization called Building Champions that provides coaches for people trying to create a work/life balance. To be honest, I only hired him because I wanted to triple the size of my company again. It was a purely selfish motive and I knew Dan could help me get the job done.

The third time Dan and I met he asked me to join him and his son for drinks after. His son was just out of college and trying to make it in the film industry. We talked for a while about movies, about how hard it is to break into the industry, when I noticed something remarkable being passed back and forth between Dan and his son. It was something like encouragement, but it was deeper and more meaningful than a kind of slap on the back. Dan was telling his son who he was, over and over there at the table. He would turn to me and talk about how talented his son was, how much courage he had. He told stories about trips he'd taken, adventures he'd gone on, and skills he'd developed. And as we kept talking, Dan mentioned his wife, how healthy she was and how she'd created a philosophy of nutrition ten years before that was only just now coming into vogue. I realized sitting there that Dan, while tender and loving toward his family, also approached his job as a husband and father the way a coach approaches a team. It occurred to me then what Dan was doing: he was building something. He was building something into the hearts of each member of his family. That perspective became attractive to me. I like building things.

One thing that surprised me working with Dan is that when it came time to build my business, we didn't start with a business plan. We started with a life plan. Dan said unless I had healthy relationships, I was doomed. He said he had thirty coaches working beneath him and they coached hundreds of executives who were worth billions of dollars and not one of them, in the history of his coaching business, could sustain any kind of success if their relational lives were unhealthy.

"What kind of marriage do you want with Betsy?" Dan asked me.

"What do you mean?" I asked.

"What do you want your marriage to look like?" he repeated.

I'd never thought about it. I'd spent countless hours detailing my business plan, my brand strategy, and even my personal life plan, but I'd never sat down to create a vision for Betsy's and my relationship. Dan said the next time we met he'd like to see a brief description of what I'd like our relationship to look like five years down the road.

The whole thing reminded me of a conversation I'd had with my friend Al Andrews. Al is a counselor with a practice in Nashville. We were driving once when I confessed to him I'd hung out the previous week with a girl I probably shouldn't be hanging out with. She was in a bad marriage and had leaned a little too much on me and I confessed I liked it. I liked playing the wise, kind counselor and yet at the same time it felt unwise and even wrong. Al sat there and nodded and didn't have the slightest look of judgment on his face. Finally, when I finished rambling, he said, "Don, all relationships are teleological."

I asked him what the word *teleological* meant.

"It means they're going somewhere," Al said. "All relationships are living and alive and moving and becoming something. My question to you," Al said seriously, "is, where is the relationship you've started with this woman going?"

I knew the answer to that question immediately. It wasn't going anywhere good. Within months, I'd be this married woman's surrogate husband, the man she could talk to, and as a man, I'd likely turn that into something physical and then I'd be a best-selling author in an extramarital affair. There's no question that's where it was going, and on an honest day I'd say that's where I wanted it to go. I ended it immediately and the last I heard she and her husband were working things out and doing well. I probably would have destroyed their marriage if I hadn't gotten honest.

I used to have a tennis coach in college who'd remind us, every time we practiced, that if you're coasting you're

going downhill. What he meant was unless we're practicing we're getting worse. And I think something like
that is true in relationships too. I think we can fall into
reactionary patterns in relationships rather than under-
standing they're things we build and nurture and grow.

What Daniel was trying to do by having me write
down a vision for my marriage was take responsibility
for where it was going. I'd made the mistake of becoming a reactionary in my relational life. I let friendships,
business relationships, and even my relationship with
Betsy take a natural course rather than guiding them to
a healthy place.

ABOUT THIS TIME I HAPPENED TO BE ATTENDING A
business retreat. Betsy and I were only able to get a few
minutes on the phone each night as I was sitting in lec-
tures and seminars all day. One night while walking
along the golf course and talking to Betsy on the phone,
catching up on our days, I noticed there was a lot of tension in Betsy's voice. She was upset about something she
normally wouldn't be upset about. I'd even say she was a
little angry with me.

You should know Betsy and I aren't a dramatic
couple. Betsy is a master at disarming tension, which
is a characteristic that will serve me the rest of my life.

Regardless, though, I hung up having no idea what I'd done wrong. I felt accused and disrespected.

The next day I attended a workshop on creating a ninety-day business plan. The workshop leader gave us a form we could fill out that would generate focus in a team and get everybody on track to increase productivity. It took me about three minutes to fill out the form for my business, but then I had an idea. I asked the workshop leader for another form, and I crossed out the word business and wrote the word marriage. I then wrote a vision statement for our marriage. I wanted our marriage to be a restorative marriage, and I wrote down some core values Betsy and I could live by. I wrote down we'd be a couple that didn't do the math in our relationship, meaning we'd avoid the temptation to think about who owes the other what. I wrote down the goal of creating a home where people could come and be restored, and a place she and I could walk into and feel safe and comfortable—not just because of the furniture, but because we'd be intentional about restoring whatever the world had done to tear us down. I wrote that with the money we spent we'd always ask whether what we were buying would help us restore each other or restore other people. Everything in our marriage would be about restoration.

I took a picture of the sheet and e-mailed it to Betsy.

I asked her to tell me what she thought, whether the marriage plan made sense and to tell me what she'd like to change about it. I didn't so much care what the plan was, but I knew enough about life to know if there's no plan, the chances of success are limited.

After e-mailing her the image, I felt dumb. All she wanted was to connect, and here I was sending her a marriage plan as though a relationship works like a business. To my surprise, though, Betsy wrote back immediately. She was ecstatic. She was relieved and thankful.

Later when Betsy and I talked about it, I realized I hadn't thought about all the fears Betsy was dealing with since we got engaged. She was about to leave DC to head to New Orleans, where, two months later, we'd be married. She was leaving a community she'd spent eight years building. She was leaving her job, her furniture, her routines, her bank account, and her incredible roommates who'd become as close as sisters. And she was leaving it all for what? She was leaving it for some guy she'd fallen in love with, some author her friends had read. She had no idea what her new life would look like. She had no idea where I was taking her. She was scared to death.

I would never walk into my office without a plan. As the leader of my company, my team depends on me to know where we are going and how important each of them are to the journey. I can't believe I almost went into my marriage, which is infinitely more important than my business, without a plan.

What happened in our relationship reminds me of a lesson I learned when I took a course to get my motorcycle license. Our instructor said that often, when we get into trouble, the bike returns to stability when you roll back the throttle and speed up. He said when we felt unstable to pick a safe place in the distance, hit the gas, and let the bike find its balance again. A motorcycle has a way of stabilizing itself under thrust.

I think that's all my relationship with Betsy needed. We hit a moment of instability and tension and we needed to pick a point on the horizon and start moving toward it. I wonder if what might help couples build great families is to pick a place for their family to go and then hit the gas, to work toward their vision and build it out. Relationships have a way of stabilizing when in motion. Until then, they just feel like a road trip to nowhere. Al was right: relationships are teleological.

THE KIND OF INTIMATE COMMUNITY MEN HELP CRE-ate in relationships had been modeled for Betsy since childhood. She's the oldest of seven children, and connection and communication are important values for her family.

The first time I met them was at Thanksgiving dinner. Betsy had never brought a guy home during the holidays, so the family was excited. She greeted me in the driveway and we walked to the back of the house, a well-forested few acres just off the north shore of Lake Pontchartrain, across the long causeway from New Orleans. All the kids are older now: one brother is a pilot in the air force, her younger sisters are professionals at a large insurance firm, and her two youngest brothers were wrapping up college. Like I said, Betsy is the oldest of seven, and both her mother and father come from large families. There seemed to be people everywhere. Happy people.

We talked for a while—the conversation, I would later learn, strictly regulated by a briefing Betsy gave the family before I arrived. There would be no talk of my books, no talk of politics, and absolutely no questions about my intentions, at least not yet. I think the boys had been teasing her. It all went perfectly, though, and after a couple of hours we pulled folding tables from the back deck and set out plates and napkins for extended family. Flowers came in from the yard to be set on tables. The doorbell began to ring and I don't think it stopped ringing for an hour. By the time we prayed for the meal, more than fifty members of the extended family had joined us, each of them curious about the man Betsy had chosen, each of the men being pinched in the side by their wives if they asked anything overly inquisitive.

Coming from a family where there were so few men, it felt foreign but right to have men at every table, husbands next to every wife. Every screaming child had a father to pick them up. Betsy's grandfather offered the blessing and her father cut the turkey. There were stories about hunting, guns misfiring, fish being caught, boats being capsized. The women seemed beautiful in contrast to the strength of the men. When we were done, we played volleyball in the backyard and football in the front. It was the old men against the young and the young men may have won, but all the trash-talking was being done by the old guys, and they were quite good at it.

Everything I'd come to love about Betsy started to make sense. I was seeing where her beauty, her patience, and her wisdom had come from. It made sense then that when we experienced tension she made respectful comments and then brought up the subject again when the moment was right. It made sense she expected me to respect and protect her. It made sense she expected me to care about relationships, about reconciliation and intentional community. This was the soil from which she'd grown.

I'd dig deeper into that soil myself when I finally

moved to New Orleans before the wedding. The family borrowed a camping trailer from a friend and set it up a few hundred yards from the house. I lived out of the trailer the six weeks before we were married, using the bathroom and showering in the house, but returning every night to my bed, a pop-out canvas contraption protruding from the back hatch of the trailer. Lucy, and I would lie there at night, wondering about what we'd gotten ourselves into. I'd lay my hand against the canvas tent to feel the raindrops and wonder if I could build a family as strong as Betsy's.

What I learned during that six weeks would be a foundation for our marriage. Betsy's dad, Ed, believed in the power of relationships. He'd served as a vice president at one of the area's largest companies before starting a home-based business. He'd built a successful career cultivating relationships and caring for clients. But none of his business relationships mattered as much as the community that really made him strong, his family first and then his friends.

And I haven't even told you the best part. The best part is Betsy's parents had recently adopted a fifteen-month-old baby. They'd been her foster parents since she was born and after falling in love with her decided to adopt her. Their youngest were already in college, yet feeling a connection with the baby decided to start over.

It wasn't an easy decision, but she'd become part of the family and they couldn't let her go.

Honestly, I learned more from the new baby than any of the others. It all goes back to the thing I was talking about in the beginning, about wanting intimacy but settling for applause. I saw it in the baby too. She's a wiggle worm, a screamer and giggler, a pass-around baby always grabbing noses. And she can't bear to be alone. She must have your attention and if she can't get it, she screams so loud she earned the nickname Teakettle.

I've met people who, well into their adult years, can't stand not being the center of attention. It's as though, like the baby, they are grabbing your face, looking you in the eye, and saying, Look at me, I'm here, do you notice me, do I matter, am I worth your sacrifice?

But in the six weeks I was at Betsy's parents' house we began to notice the baby was calming down. The screaming wasn't as loud or as often. And she was able to walk onto the porch by herself exploring her world, forgetting for minutes at a time she wasn't the center of attention. The love was healing and she was changing because of it. Soon she'd grow into a child who could not only receive love but give it back to those asking the same questions we are all asking: Do I matter? Am I worth your sacrifice?

I don't know that I've seen a healthier place to have those questions answered than the home Betsy grew up in. The house was a revolving door of kids coming home for the weekend and extended family stopping by for a visit. Relationships were so important to her father that while I was there he rented space from a local retreat center and brought in a speaker to teach a course on how relationships work. All the kids came back home for the retreat and about twenty friends of the family joined as well. Who does that? Who hosts their own retreat to improve the relationships they have with their friends and family?

You'd think all this talk about relationships would create a sentimental, mushy environment, but it didn't. Instead it created a foundational strength from which each family member would build their lives. Betsy's siblings were doing well. They were healthy and impactful in their communities. The family was working. It was doing what a family was supposed to do, converting potentially neglected kids into relationally competent and satisfied adults able to give back to people and create a better world.

Since I first discovered how remarkable Betsy was I've felt a certain responsibility. I no longer believe God is working behind the scenes to make me powerful, rich, or famous. Instead, I think I'm supposed to contribute something to the people around me and create an environment where healthy relationships can flourish.

I don't mind saying that intimacy and family began to feel more like a project than a sentiment—and the more I saw it as a project, something meaningful to build, the more I got excited about it. Like I said, men like to build and create and feel their power, and if they don't do it in healthy ways they usually do it in unhealthy ways. I was seeing an empire of rich, healthy relationships and I wanted to build an empire of my own.

AT NIGHT, AFTER HANGING OUT WITH THE FAMILY, I'd walk the path to my camper and light a fire in the pit they'd put out under the awning. Lucy would lie beside the fire, looking for squirrels or creatures heading to the pond for a drink. Betsy's dad would come out and have a glass of whiskey with me before bed. One night when we were sitting out there he made a comment about the fire. He said if we took the logs from the fire and separated them out in the field, they'd go out within an hour. They'd just lie there cold. He said for some reason the logs needed each other to burn, to stay warm.

I don't think he meant anything other than to talk about the fire, but looking across the field back toward the house, I realized how beautiful what he and his wife had built was and how hard they'd worked to keep the fire going. I wanted to build a fire like that of my own.

15

You Will Not Complete Me

WHEN I WAS A KID I REMEMBER SEEING THE MOVIE *Jerry Maguire.* There is a famous scene in the movie in which Jerry Maguire tells Dorothy Boyd that she completes him. That scene was all the rage back then and couples everywhere were saying it to each other in coffee shops and bars. Even I thought it was a beautiful sentiment. But now that I'm older and smarter, I have a new name for it: codependency.

I didn't know anything about codependency before going to Onsite, and even after I heard it defined I didn't realize I struggled with it myself, but I did. And it cost me relationship after relationship.

Codependency happens when too much of your sense of validation or security comes from somebody else. Now that I know what it is, I can spot it pretty easily. If somebody obsesses over whether another person likes them or returns an e-mail or whatever, it's a symptom of codependency, though a mild one. Stalking would be a scarier version of the same tendency.

I've a close friend who is a love addict. He goes from girl to girl ruining relationships by smothering them. What he doesn't realize is that no amount of love any of those girls returns is going to heal the hole in his heart.

Back at Onsite, our group therapist created a terrific visual example of what a healthy relationship looks like. She put three pillows on the floor and asked a couple of us to stand on the pillows. She told us to leave the middle pillow open. She pointed at my pillow and said, "Don, that's your pillow, that's your life. The only person who gets to step on that pillow is you. Nobody else. That's your territory, your soul." Then she pointed at my friend's pillow and told her that was her pillow, that she owned it and it was her soul. Then, the therapist said, the middle pillow symbolized the relationship.

She said that both of us could step into the middle pillow any time we wanted because we'd agreed to be in a relationship. However, she said, at no point is it appropriate to step on the other person's pillow. What goes on in the other person's soul is none of your business. All you're responsible for is your soul, nobody else's. Regarding the middle pillow, the question to ask is, "What do I want in a relationship?" If the pillow you two step on together works, that's great. If not, move on or simply explain what you'd like life to feel like in the middle pillow and see if the other person wants that kind of relationship too. But never, she said, ever try to change each other. Know who you are and know what you want in a relationship, and give people the freedom to be themselves.

I wish I'd have heard that in my twenties. I can't tell you how many girls' pillows I've stomped on trying to get them to change. And the sleepless nights I've spent wondering what they were thinking or how much they liked me or whether I was a good enough man for them. A complete waste of time.

At one point, while working with our group therapist, I mentioned that if I did such and such a thing the girl I was seeing might think, blah blah blah. She stopped the session and asked me why I spent so much time wondering what other people were thinking.

"That's going to drive you crazy, Don," she said. "Just ask yourself if you're happy and what you want in a relationship and that's it. What's going on in other people's minds is none of your business."

Suddenly I felt like a Peeping Tom of the soul, going through the neighborhood looking in the windows of people's souls wondering what they were doing in there. And just like that, a habit I'd developed decades before felt creepy.

IN A WAY, THAT'S THE DIFFERENCE BETWEEN MY relationship with Betsy and my relationships with all the other girls. Because I know which pillow is mine and which pillow is hers, I hold Betsy loosely. If she wants to leave she can go. I'm responsible for my own health and happiness, and I'm responsible to ask what I want in a relationship and to try to make the middle pillow comfortable and safe for her, but that's it. Of course we will stand and make promises to each other at our wedding but even then, even with a spouse, I've come to believe a person's love for you can't grow unless you hold that person loosely.

And that feels good. Unlike every other girl I've dated, I've never wondered where Betsy was or who she was with. I've never looked at her phone, and I've never looked at her Facebook page. Her life is her life and mine is mine and what we have together is a relationship. And it's great.

I don't want you to misunderstand me: I love Betsy more than any woman I've ever met and I believe I always will. But this is a healthy love, not the needy love I've experienced in the past. Before, I'd try to control whoever I loved so she couldn't get away. Much of it was passive control, but it was there all the same. I used fear and guilt and shame to close my fingers around my girlfriend's heart, and without exception I killed whatever love could have grown.

I now know there were two dominant influences that caused me to clench my fist. The first was the fact I was trying to use women to heal old wounds, and the second was the false assumption I could be made complete by any of these women in the first place.

THE REVELATION THAT I HAD BEEN USING WOMEN to heal old wounds helped me understand where the codependency characteristic came from. I realized what was going on when I read a book called *Getting the Love You Want* by Dr. Harville Hendrix. It's a more clinical book than its title suggests, but Hendrix' theory struck home. Essentially he argues that on a subconscious level we are drawn to the negative characteristics of our primary caretakers. What he means is that when we were children we had parents and older siblings and grandparents and perhaps even teachers with whom we associated our basic needs for survival. In other words, if we didn't please our parents and grandparents, our food, shelter, and love were under threat.

Hendrix believes when we meet somebody later in life who exhibits some of the negative characteristics of those early foundational personalities, our subconscious recognizes them as the Mommy or Daddy with whom we have unfinished business. Literally, our brains become attached to this random person thinking if we could just fix some of those negative qualities in ourselves we could have security and never worry about food, shelter, or love again. That's why guys who grew up with controlling mothers are often drawn to controlling women, and girls who grew up with abusive fathers are often drawn to men who treat them similarly. It's a rather sad theory, actually.

But as crazy as it sounds, it made sense. I'd spent a lifetime being drawn to women who exhibited some of the patterns I'd grown up with. And more than that, what I'd misunderstood as passion or love was actually a deep sense that if this relationship worked out, my oldest wounds might be healed. In other words, I didn't love these girls so much as I wanted to use them to fix something broken inside of me. And because of that incredible need, I'd step all over their pillows for fear of losing them.

It's interesting how much just being aware of this dynamic began to change the nature of my relationships. Suddenly I was able to see why I was drawn to a person and decide, apart from whatever fireworks were going off in my subconscious, whether or not this could be a healthy relationship. And most of the time it couldn't. I suddenly had the power to walk away before anybody got hurt. And soon enough that old attraction mechanism faded away almost completely. I just wasn't drawn to the same kinds of women.

Oddly, Hendrix argues, the more a partner exhibits the negative characteristics of our primary caretakers the more passion we will experience in the relationship. At first I found this to be a sad reality but truthfully, in time, I started to see the deception inherent in the primal emotion we often mistake for love. When I met couples whose marriages were thriving after thirty and forty years, none of them were riding an emotional roller coaster of passion and then resentment. Instead, they loved each other as an act of their conscious will. They were more in control of their love than their "love" was in control of them.

That's why I think it took Betsy and me a little longer to fall in love. She simply didn't have any of the negative characteristics I had once been subconsciously attracted to. I remember sitting across from her on one of our first dates, noting her incredible beauty but also wondering whether we could work out because I didn't feel in love. It occurred to me then I hadn't known her long enough to feel in love in the first place. I'm not saying a couple can't experience love at first sight. I'm only saying sooner or later that love will have to encounter the hard facts of reality. Does this person have the kind of character and discipline it takes to make a loving relationship work? Is the passion real or are they trying to heal old wounds?

Over time, my feelings grew but they weren't the old feelings of obsession. They were more like respect, admiration, and attraction. Betsy seemed to have everything it took to go the distance. She was beautiful, respectful, strong, and kind. She was a master at resolving conflict and had absolutely no skill at manipulation. In fact, I'd say the thing that caused me to truly fall in love with her was quite practical: I realized there wasn't another girl on the planet with whom I was more compatible to have a healthy relationship, and if there was another girl, I never wanted to meet her.

ANOTHER PARADIGM SHIFT THAT ALLOWED ME TO finally have a healthy relationship was theological. I realized there was a subconscious longing in my heart that could never be resolved by another human being. Certainly Betsy could resolve my longing for an intimate companion, but I'm talking about something deeper. Some people think of it as the longing for God, and I think they're on to something. In my opinion, though, that longing will never be satisfied in our lifetime. In other words, I'm convinced every person has a longing that will never be fulfilled and it's our job to let it live and breathe and suffer within it as a way of developing our character.

I remember growing up in church hearing about how there was a hole in our hearts that could only be filled by Jesus, but later in life when I became a Jesus guy myself I continued to experience the longing. He simply wasn't doing it. The experience was so frustrating I almost walked away from faith.

Later, though, I read in the Bible about how there will be a wedding in heaven and how, someday, we will be reunited with God. The Bible paints a beautiful picture of a lion lying down with a lamb, of all our tears being wiped away, of a mediator creating peace and a King ruling with wisdom and kindness. The language is scattered and often vague, but there's no question something in the souls of men will be healed and perhaps even made complete once we are united with God and not a second before. What differentiates true Christianity from the pulp many people buy into is that Jesus never offers that completion here on earth. He only asks us to trust him and follow him to the metaphorical wedding we will experience in heaven.

The more I thought about it, the more the Bible made sense. Early followers of Jesus experienced pain and trial and frustration, hardly the romantic life. But they consoled each other and took care of each other and comforted each other in the longing.

In my opinion the misappropriation of the longing for God has caused a lot of people a great deal of pain. In fact, I wondered if some of my early mistakes in relationships weren't partly because I sought to find resolution for the longing through a woman, a burden no romantic partner should have to bear. How many relationships have been ruined by two people attempting to squeeze the Jesus out of each other?

Early in our relationship Betsy and I talked about this dynamic and decided we wouldn't fall for it. We knew we would each experience an unresolved longing neither of us would be able to fulfill. We came to see this as a positive rather than a negative. The fact we couldn't be tricked into resenting each other for not healing each other's deepest wounds might be the difference between our relationship and the many that have crashed and burned.

I'll never forget the night before our wedding, though, when I tried to explain this idea to our friends and family. I nearly blew it. More than a hundred people came to the rehearsal dinner. When it was time to give the final toast, I stood before our friends and family and confessed Betsy and I didn't believe we completed each other. I didn't think about how odd it would sound, but the room looked back at me silently as though I were announcing a breakup.

I quickly explained the reason I thought we were so healthy was because neither of us put unfair expectations on each other. Some of the women in the room were looking at me like I was the least romantic man in the world. Betsy just looked at me and laughed. I attempted to recover, stammering about how our deepest longings will someday be met by God. I talked about what the longing always felt like for me, how it's a longing for ultimate acceptance, to be one with something greater than myself, something I've sensed casts a reflection in the beauty of the ocean or the grandeur of the mountains. I talked about how I've always felt the longing and Betsy has always felt it too.

"Betsy and I are going to try as hard as we can not

to put the burden of that longing on each other," I said. "Instead, we will comfort each other in the longing and even love it for what it is, a promise that God will someday fulfill us."

I don't know how many people really understood my toast. I would imagine there were some who wondered if Betsy and I didn't think we could fulfill each other, why we'd get married in the first place. But for me, the answer to that question is simple: we both get somebody to share the longing with.

I don't know if there's a healthier way for two people to stay in love than to stop using each other to resolve their unfulfilled longings and, instead, start holding each other closely as they experience them.

I don't mind the longing. The longing is beautiful. I just don't want to feel it alone anymore. I want to share it with Betsy.

16

The Place We Left
Our Ghosts

FOR SOME, BECOMING CAPABLE OF INTIMACY IS AS
difficult as losing a hundred pounds. It involves decon-
structing old habits, overcoming the desire to please
people, telling the truth, and finding satisfaction
in a daily portion of real love. In the year leading to
our wedding, I felt like I'd lost forty of those hundred
pounds but I had a long way to go. A few months before
the wedding, though, I watched something happen that
gave me hope.

The venue Betsy chose was an old, neglected country club along the banks of the Tchefuncte River. She'd chosen it while I was off on a writing retreat. She explained on the phone that the price was right but it needed help, a considerable amount of help. I asked why she wanted to get married in a place that wasn't perfect, and she told me *perfect is subjective*. She said her family had memories there, that her grandparents had a home along the golf course and her mother grew up swimming in the pool behind the ballroom. She described the setting more like a story than a place. She said we could get married in a large space next to the swimming pool across from a hundred-year-old oak. There would be lanterns along the edge of the pool leading down to a dock floating long and low into the river. I asked if we could leave the wedding by boat and she loved the idea.

When I returned to New Orleans Betsy took me to the venue. We drove through the neighborhood, winding our way through homes set on half-acre plots divided to protect the ancient oaks more than to evenly divide the land. There were tall, concrete columns holding gothic statues marking the gates to the old club. The oaks spread over the gray walls where they dropped their leaves so they crunched under our tires. The gate to the country club was broken and open, leaning heavy on the parking lot as though still proud of the protection it once gave. I could feel the history of the place as we drove. And I understood why Betsy wanted to add our wedding to that history. Across the river were trees growing out of the swamp as tall as a forest for giants. It was the best of New Orleans. You got the feeling its ghosts were pleasant. Even in the parking lot there was an ancient oak flowing tufts of hanging moss like the long, soft beards of old men.

But when we walked into the courtyard I had a sudden change of mind. It was worse than she'd let on.

Betsy moved without speaking, hoping I could see what she saw. But I couldn't. I saw weeds growing through the cracks in the concrete and broken bricks fallen and piled along the flower beds. The bench around the great oak had missing planks, and the swimming pool, once enjoyed by her mother, was brown turning black. Tadpoles as large as catfish darted into the center as we approached and a turtle tilted its shell into the murk, flapping a leg toward the surface as it sank.

I tried not to show my surprise and began to strategize how we could get out of the contract. Because I didn't want to let on my dismay, I asked Betsy to talk me through what she was thinking. She walked slowly, speaking softly. She said the pool would be cleaned, of course. And we'd have a tent between the pool and the ballroom where people could sit comfortably under heaters. She said her aunt had a hundred lanterns and showed me where they'd round the pool and light a path to the dock. She showed me where we would stand to say our vows, the guests facing us with the oak as a backdrop and the river bending off into the distance beyond the tree. She said the sun would set behind the oak and her brother-in-law would sit here to play the guitar. She said, "This is where your mother will say the prayer, and this is where Matt and Bob will officiate the ceremony."

Part of me wanted to explain it was too much to fix. But if Betsy had taught me anything it was that there was never a reason to overreact. She's the queen of sifting softness over drama. She could see the concern on my face, so she talked reverently about what the place had been and what it could be again if we'd only pour some love into it. She told a story about her uncle visiting the pool as a boy, too poor to afford a swimsuit. He swam in jean shorts and all the girls giggled. He said for years the place made him feel less than. That is until he married one of the girls. I smiled at that. It's funny how a story can start to remodel a place.

As I thought about our guests, as I thought about Bob giving the homily and our parents having prayed for our partners even before we were born, it became difficult to walk away from the challenge. What phase of this courtship hadn't needed a miracle anyway? And why not participate in one more?

Betsy looked at me hopefully and I reluctantly agreed this is where we'd be married. She walked over, leaned her head on my shoulder, and laid her fingers in my hand. We stood and watched the sun set beyond the pool, Betsy remembering so many beautiful scenes from her childhood while I sniffed the air and wondered if the pool weren't also being used as a bathroom for vagabonds.

Each time we'd go back to visit the place the pool had been drained a little more, more of the weeds were gone, and another load of debris had been hauled away. It would still take a miracle, but you could see how the story we were living was starting to bear fruit in the real world. Something was being renewed.

I was getting caught up in the story too. Betsy would be talking to the property manager or the wedding coordinator and I'd suddenly sense the depth of it all. I say sense because there's no rational explanation for that kind of emotion except perhaps, at times, we accidentally tear a little hole in the fabric of reality so something on the other side shines through, exposing the darkness of our routine existence. More than once when we visited the country club I had to walk away from Betsy and the wedding coordinator because I was getting tears in my eyes.

My friend Al Andrews was right. Relationships are teleological. They're all going somewhere and they're turning us into something, hopefully something better, something new. What Betsy was doing to the place was no different than what our relationship was doing to me. What else changes a person but the living of a story? And what is a story but the wanting for something difficult and the willingness to work for it?

I ONCE HEARD SOMEBODY SAY WOMEN MARRY A man but men marry a season. I think there's a little truth in that. Had the sun not set on the season of my singleness, I never would have done the work it took to try toward intimacy. But it was time and I was ready.

I think it's harder for marriages to work out these days than it's ever been. We all need more of a miracle now than we used to. Guys grow up much later and the patterns we learn are unhealthy. I had little doubt, even as we chose the wedding cake and the caterers and the ties my groomsmen would wear, that marriage was going to be a challenge. Certainly it would be enjoyable, but when a writer with a tendency to isolate partners with an extrovert who loves to practice hospitality, the stuff of story ensues. And stories are all about conflict.

What lies between a person and what that person wants is work. And I'd done the work. Or at least I started the work. The old me was slowly dying into the new me, the one compatible for intimacy. And this slow death and resurrection will likely last the rest of my life.

I no longer believe love works like a fairy tale but like farming. Most of it is just getting up early and tilling the soil and then praying for rain. But if we do the work, we just might wake up one day to find an endless field of crops rolling into the horizon. In my opinion, that's even better than a miracle. I'd rather earn the money than win the lottery because there's no joy in a reward unless it comes at the end of a story.

THE POOL WAS CLEAN JUST IN TIME. THE TURTLES had been thrown back into the river, the tadpoles were scooped into nets, and God only knows how many hours of pressure-washing were applied to make the place look new. The guy who tended the property hid a hose on the backside of the gothic fountain to make it look like it was working and we set lamps on the broken benches around the oak so nobody would sit on them. Betsy's uncle Charlie happened to own a nursery and brought in a hundred trees and shrubs, and Betsy's brothers set them in front of broken bricks or chipped paint. Another of Betsy's uncles pulled a boat up to the dock and her aunts decorated it with streamers and signs announcing our marriage. My groomsmen and Betsy's brothers bought fireworks and placed them on the dock so they could light them as we made our escape. It's encouraging to watch what people will do to contribute to a love story. It's as though we universally recognize the union of souls is worth sacrificing for.

I remember my friend John telling me once about how long it took him to marry his wife. He said they dated for nine years before he finally gave in. It's not that he didn't want to marry her. He always did. It's just that he kept waiting for it to feel a certain way. Twice, while walking into a jewelry store to pick out an engagement ring, he had a panic attack and crawled out, clutching his chest. Finally, a friend of his who is a therapist pulled him aside and explained love was a decision, that it was as much something you made happen as it was something that happened to you. John finally acknowledged both the single and married life had its rewards, but in the end he'd rather be with his wife. He said he made the decision and his wedding day was the happiest day of his life.

I felt the same. Our wedding was the end of a wonderful adventure that took me through dark places and brought me toward a greater light. And of course it would be the beginning of a much harder adventure. My faith teaches me that the path to join souls in love must of necessity involve a crucifixion, and I think there's a metaphor in there for marriage.

I've heard it said that it's a man's job to rescue a woman, but I didn't feel like I was rescuing anybody that day. I felt as though I were the one who was being rescued, rescued from my fear and insecurity that made me so frighteningly poor at relationships, rescued from isolation and from fairy-tale illusions about what love really is. And it wasn't just Betsy who rescued me. It was God and my friends and my therapists and a chorus of characters who wanted to see love win the day.

About an hour before the wedding, Bob walked over and put his hand on my shoulder. He looked at me and said, "Don, you're good at relationships." I still don't know if he's completely right. I have a lot of work to do and I know marriage is hard. But when Bob said it this time it felt more true than it ever had. I really did get better.

I suppose that's the point of this book. There's truth in the idea we're never going to be perfect in love but we can get close. And the closer we get, the healthier we will be. Love is not a game any of us can win, it's just a story we can live and enjoy. It's a noble ambition, then, to add a chapter to the story of love, and to make our chapter a good one.

We don't think much about how our love stories will affect the world, but they do. Children learn what's worth living for and what's worth dying for by the stories they watch us live. I want to teach our children how to get scary close, and more, how to be brave. I want to teach them that love is worth what it costs.

Much of the rest of the wedding is a blur to me now. I do remember the beards of the old men in the oak leaning toward our tent to watch the ceremony, and the glowing faces of our friends and family, and Betsy in her dress stepping out the country-club doors into the courtyard, beaming like a light so seldom seen, shining through the torn fabric of the world like a rare glimpse of grace.

I am so grateful.

To see pictures of Don and Betsy's wedding,
visit www.scaryclose.com

Acknowledgments

I'M GRATEFUL TO BETSY MILLER FOR BEING MY partner in the endless journey of intimacy and for risking on the "black box" investment that is human love. I'm also thankful for her incredible family, the Miltenbergers. I'm grateful to her parents, Ed and Laurie, whose adventure wasn't an ocean or a mountain but a family. You've built something deeper, wider, and taller than the isolated conqueror could dream of and we are all blessed for your work. Thanks also to my mother who gave me the gift of safety and without whom I'd not feel comfortable revealing myself or my story to the world.

An enormous number of friends loaned me their stories and wisdom. I'm grateful for Paul and Kim Young, Mark, Jon, and Tim Foreman, Henry Cloud, John Cotton Richmond, Marshall and Jamie Allman, David Gentiles and his daughters, Al Andrews, the Miltenberger family, Dr. Harville Hendrix, Daniel Harkavy, Ben and Elaine Pearson, and John and Terri MacMurray.

I wrote this book with a great deal of help from editors. I'm grateful to Joel Miller, Jennifer Stair, and Heather Skelton. Their tireless work on getting the bugs out of this manuscript was invaluable to me. I'm also grateful for the marketing and publicity team at Thomas Nelson. Thanks to Belinda Bass, Chad Cannon, and the entire team. I also want to thank Shauna Niequist who carefully read through the manuscript and gave invaluable feedback, and for Bryan Norman, an amazing literary agent who carefully read the book and gave me more than 100 pages of "notes in the margin." I'm truly grateful.

I'd also like to thank Brian Hampton, my publisher, with whom I've been working for many years now. Brian has been patient, wise, and kind, and without his counsel I doubt I'd have been able to shape this book.

Betsy and I thank our friends at Onsite Workshops and their Living Centered Program. Without their unique way of helping people and the incredible friendships we made with Miles Adcox and Bill and Laurie Lokey, I'd likely still be lost.

Without the staff at StoryBrand I'd never have been given the time to write this book. They keep things moving. Thanks to Tim Schurrer, Kyle Reid, Kyle Hicks, and Cadence Turpin for making the office feel like a home.

Thanks also to our friends who offered their beautiful songs to the soundtrack. Thanks for sharing your hearts and your talents and for giving us the anthems that somehow bind us in a common experience of beauty.

I also want to thank Bob Goff, who kept telling me I was good at relationships and without whom this story would have no arc. Thanks for being such a faithful friend for so many years. You're good at relationships too.

And finally, I'm thankful to you. I've been at this a long time now and wouldn't be able to do this without you. Though I write with the voice of a memoirist, my goal is to tell the collective story we share. In some mysterious way, I hope this connects us to one another. That connection has been healing for me and I'm thankful.

About the Author

DONALD MILLER IS THE AUTHOR OF SEVERAL BOOKS, including the bestsellers *Blue Like Jazz* and *A Million Miles in a Thousand Years*. He helps people live a better story at www.creatingyourlifeplan.com and has a marketing consulting company at www.storybrand.com.

The Next Step

MEANINGFUL RELATIONSHIPS

3 online courses to help you
become a more loving person

PRE-MARRIAGE

MARRIAGE

PARENTING